The Myth of Race

Our DNA Defines Who We Are

By

Thomas C. Spelsberg Ph.D.

Copyright © 2011 by Thomas C. Spelsberg Ph.D.

Thomas C. Spelsberg, Ph.D.
The Myth of Race: Our DNA Defines Who We Are
ISBN: 0-6154-4030-4

Web page: www.themythofrace.com

Publisher: TCS Scientific

Text design by Jacquelyn House
Illustrations by Ken Peters and Thomas Spelsberg Ph.D.
Editor: Katie Spelsberg
Production editor: Nancy Spelsberg
Cover design by Shilpa Gajarawala
Date printed: 2011

Acknowledgements

The author wishes to acknowledge the following individuals for the preparation of the book: Karen Herman of the Mayo Clinic Alumni office who inspired and encouraged me to prepare lectures on this topic (The Myth of Race); my daughter, Nancy Spelsberg, and wife, Liza Spelsberg, for encouraging me to put the lecture into a book form; Ken Peters, who designed many of the excellent illustrations the author had sketched; Jacquelyn House for her excellent clerical assistance; the proof readers of the book who provided excellent suggestions for revisions of this book: Nancy Spelsberg (Engineer); Katie Spelsberg (Science Teacher); Elizabeth Spelsberg (Elementary Teacher); Kelly Withers Behnke (Legal Assistant); Sarah Spelsberg (Physician Assistant), Ayalew Tefferi, M.D. (Clinical Staff in Hematology and Oncology at the Mayo Clinic); Eric Wieben, Ph.D. (Staff Scientist in Molecular Genetics at the Mayo Clinic); Brian Davies, Ph.D. (Scientist in Biochemistry and Molecular Biology at the Mayo Clinic), and Jim Ashenmacher (Information Technology).

Outline

Title Page	i
Publishing	ii
Acknowledgements	iii
Outline	v
Professional Biography of the Author	vii
Abstract of Book	xi
Preface	xv

Chapters

1.	Introduction and the History of Race and Racism	3
2.	The Origins of Modern Humans	15
3.	The Human Genome: The Genetic Material that Makes Us Who We Are	23
4.	Using Polymorphisms to Track Human Origins and World Migrations	43
5.	Why and How Do Populations Become Different: The Role of Isolation and Environment	69
6.	Biology and Genetics Say We Are Only Variants of One Species	91
7.	The Myth of Race	105

Glossary 111

Appendices

I. Notes for further reading 119
II. Expanded descriptions of mutations, polymorphisms, and genetic drift 131
III. References, resources and further reading 139
IV. Some interesting facts about human history 143
V. Some companies for gene analysis 145

Professional Biography of the Author

Thomas C. Spelsberg, Ph.D., has been on staff at the Mayo Clinic for over 36 years. He is a Named Professor of Biochemistry and Molecular Biology and a Mayo Distinguished Investigator. He was born and raised in Clarksburg, West Virginia and received his BA and Ph.D. from West Virginia University in Genetics and Biochemistry. He then became a fellow and subsequently a faculty member, in the Department of Biochemistry at the University of Texas M.D. Anderson Hospital and Tumor Institute, Houston, TX. He subsequently joined the faculty of Reproductive Biology at Vanderbilt Medical Center in 1970 and, while there, was awarded a National Genetics Foundation Scholarship. He joined the Mayo Clinic in 1973 in the Department of Biochemistry, Cell and Molecular Biology.

Dr. Spelsberg has served as Section Head and then Chair of the Department of Biochemistry and Molecular Biology (1988-1995). From 1984 to 1994 he served as the Director of the Mayo Clinic Center for Reproductive Biology, and served as the Principal Investigator of the NIH-funded Center for Reproductive Biology for ten years. Dr. Spelsberg holds the George M.

Eisenberg Professorship and received the first Distinguished Investigator Award from the Mayo Clinic. He has also received several teaching awards from the students of the Mayo Graduate and Medical Schools. He has mentored 65 pre- and post-doctoral fellows. In 1988 he was elected Secretary of the Officers and Councilors by the Mayo Clinic Staff and then elected in 1995 as the first Ph.D. President of the Mayo Clinic Staff. From 1999 to 2005, Dr. Spelsberg served as Mayo Clinic's Director of Medical Genomics Education Program.

Over his career, he has served on NIH review boards, national committees, advisory boards, and numerous editorial boards of scientific journals. He was elected to the Council of the American Society for Bone and Mineral Research and to the West Virginia University Academy of Distinguished Alumni, and was appointed to the National Advisory Board for the West Virginia University Health Sciences Center. He is internationally recognized for research into the mechanisms of action of steroid hormones, hormone antagonists, growth factors, and transcription factors in human breast cancer, and skeletal disease. He currently holds a dozen U.S. patents and has been awarded numerous NIH and Foundation grants over the past 4 decades.

He has authored over 350 publications, and has presented over 50 symposia and plenary lectures. Over the past 15 years, his fellows have received approximately 40 national and international awards for their research. He is a member and Past President of the Board of Directors for the George M. Eisenberg Foundation for Charities of Chicago.

Abstract of the Book

This book describes the origins and world migrations of modern man, and presents the argument that many of the concepts of the term race are a myth. The spontaneous, periodic changes in the DNA, called genetic drift, are described. Molecular anthropologists use these DNA changes, called polymorphisms, which cause genetic drift, as genetic markers to track mankind's origins, migrations, and overall ancestry. Since these changes occur with a consistent periodicity, scientists can also estimate the age of the change (i.e., occurrence of the polymorphism and thus date the migrations).

This book describes how world migrations, geographic isolations, local population expansions, and environmental selection, create ethnic groups (races) with unique genetic differences and traits. These different ethnic groups around the world display differences in appearances, as well as metabolism, including disease predisposition and resistance and other traits. If the population returns to its original location (i.e., environment) for an extended period, many of the physical and metabolic traits acquired are predicted to be reversed in that population.

Molecular anthropology has shown that no race or ethnic group is pure, and in reality, all are mixtures of many past cultures (tribes) of people. All humans in the world are African, all of us are cousins (related to one another to one degree or another), and all of us are essentially mongrels (mixed breeds). Further, all humans on the earth are variants of the same biological species (since all races and ethnic groups can produce fertile offspring). Thus, the studies of humans via molecular genetics and anthropology provide proof that many beliefs about races, racism, and racialism are societal concepts, not biological ones, and are actually myths. We are all one.

The goal of this book is to answer important questions such as: who are we humans; where did we come from; how different are we compared to each other and to other living organisms, yet how similar are we; why are there differences in appearance among the human world populations, how these occur, and are we still changing today? The final chapters include some thoughts by the author as to why certain individuals, societies, and nations follow racist views and activities involving the abuse of others. The author believes these attitudes are learned behaviors and are encouraged by 1) ignorance of the facts, 2) the need to feel superior, 3) as an excuse to create an enemy, or 4) the desire to defraud others of their possessions.

In brief, racism and racial profiling of other fellow humans are encouraged by self-serving desires and goals. It is interesting to note that individuals within any given population display greater variations than those found between populations. It is these genetically-induced metabolic differences among individual humans in a population, recently revealed by molecular genetics, that have created the new field of "Individualized Medicine." This new field of medicine more accurately defines and categorizes the unique disease predisposition in each of us, as well as the determination of more accurate, individualized treatments.

Preface

This book was inspired by the racial hatred, profiling and related violence among peoples of the earth. It is written for the youth and science-oriented adult readers with the hope to deter racial prejudices in societies. The goal is to present, in simple terms, a biological and genetic perspective of race based on exciting recent knowledge gained from the Human Genome Project and Molecular Anthropology. The book includes human origins, world migrations, and the changes in humans' appearances and metabolism which ultimately occur. The primary goal is to demonstrate how the social constructs of race are biologically wrong and a myth. The book uses figures, models, and tables, together with simple descriptions, to explain genetic ancestry and how individual differences between humans on the earth occur.

This book will hopefully excite you about these evolving new fields of molecular biology, medical genetics, and molecular anthropology, as well as educate you about where humans originated, that humans are all related, and that all humans are simply minor variants of the same species. Importantly, this book is intended to convince people that certain concepts about race are social, not biological, concepts and are fundamentally erroneous.

The book is divided into chapters, each of which starts with a list of defined terms used in that chapter. The book begins with a brief history of racism among various cultures, as well as a brief introduction to early human origins in Africa, as learned from Physical Anthropology analyses.

The book then describes the human genome (the total genetic material in a human, i.e. all the DNA), and how it compares with other genomes of other organisms and humans around the world. The next chapter describes the origins of DNA polymorphisms, how they occur, and how they are used to define who we are as individuals and as populations. This is followed by simple descriptions of how genetics and the new field of Molecular Anthropology are being used to track human origins and migrations around the world.

Subsequent chapters describe how geographic isolation, together with changing environments, create human diversity and traits (i.e. ethnic populations), and help to define human "races" worldwide. How DNA polymorphisms serve as the basis of

Individualized Medicine is also explained. The book concludes with a summation of facts describing how the concepts of racism conflict with the scientific revelations gained from Molecular Genetics, the Human Genome Project, and the field of Molecular Anthropology.

For the past 38 years, as a teacher and research scientist at the Mayo Clinic, I have often been asked to present a variety of general medical research lectures at local, national, and international clinical meetings to the Mayo staff and alumni, and to the public. These lectures ranged from genetic engineering and frontiers in medicine to medical genomics and regenerative medicine (tissue/organ regeneration), and more recently on individualized medicine. These lectures included descriptions of the use of DNA polymorphisms in characterizing human diseases and disease predispositions.

Due to my personal interests, I began to add information on a hobby of mine, Anthropology, which currently is using molecular DNA technology in tracking human origins and world migrations. Family members and staff colleagues at the Mayo Clinic encouraged the writing of this book due to the interest and need in our society to understand human diversity, who we are, where we originated, and the myriad concepts of race.

This book was developed with the hope that simple biological/genetic explanations of human origins and physical differences, in terms of the recent discoveries gained from advances in Molecular Genetics and Molecular Anthropology, will help individuals and societies worldwide to better understand ourselves as humans and our concepts of human ethnicity, race, and racism. It was inspired by the troubled history of societies in dealing with racism which still exists. Hopefully, this book will help individuals and societies deal with this issue.

Chapter 1

Introduction and the History of Race and Racism

1

Introduction and the History of Race and Racism

Definitions

Genetic Drift: The periodic, spontaneous changes over time in our DNA, some of which ultimately can cause changes in appearances/physiology in isolated populations which ultimately creates differences between populations (ethnic groups).

Molecular Anthropology: The study of mankind, comparing their physical characteristics (from physical anthropology) and habitats with differences in their DNA.

Introduction

This book, The Myth of Race: Our DNA Defines Who We Are, was finalized after much thought, study, discussions, and written revisions. The term "race" while a valid English language term, is more of a societal/cultural term and not a scientific term. The negative interpretation of ethnic groups as races by human societies, and even nations, is shown to be erroneous and without merit. This has generated negative cultural terms such as racialism, racism, racist, and racial profiling. These terms are found in the English dictionaries, but not in scientific dictionaries. Many of the concepts of race have now been shown by science to be a myth.

This book is not meant to address any controversy between creationism and evolution. In fact, many revelations from the Human Genome Project and Molecular Anthropology support historical descriptions of peoples in the Old Testament of the Christian Bible, the Hebrew Torah, and Islam's Quran. This book does address some interesting aspects of human diversity starting when modern humans seem to have appeared on earth.

I hope this book on the Myth of Race will help you gain a better perspective of what it means to be human, how we compare with other living organisms on the earth, and why various human ethnic groups around the globe look different, but, in reality, are so alike.

This book provides molecular genetic evidence, gained by scientists around the globe, that we are all one species, and only variants of the same species. Proof is also provided that 1) we are <u>all</u> African, 2) everyone is a composite of peoples from different cultures, and 3) all of us are related, cousins so to speak, at one level or another. In essence, all humans are a mix of many cultures from different geographic regions. We could be classified as "mongrels," as our canine friends are often classified. The different appearances among human ethnic groups are caused by constant genetic drift (spontaneous, periodic changes in our DNA), together with selection (positive and negative) caused by geographic isolation and the environment.

Molecular Anthropology now predicts that placing each of us in a different environment for thousands of years (200 - 1000 generations, or 4,000 - 20,000 years) can create a population with different physical appearances. This is due to a natural, spontaneous, and periodic biological process which occurs in all living organisms, including humans, called "genetic drift," and to environmental selection. Mating of migrants with the local peoples only enhances these changes. Welcome to the human race. We, as variants of a single species, are amazing organisms. Our DNA defines who we really are. We are all one.

Misuse of the term "race" occurs by a lack of knowledge or by personal agendas of individuals and societies. As quoted by Steve Olson in his book Mapping Human History, "the word race has become so burdened with misconceptions, so weighed down by social baggage, that it serves no useful purpose." Racism has occurred in human history due to a need to feel superior, as an excuse for one's behavior (jealousy) or harmful actions, or for personal gain. Feelings of distrust of foreigners (i.e., those different from oneself) possibly arose from early times, when invaders of any geographical area by foreign/different looking peoples were often a real threat. However, much of the discriminatory attitudes today are "learned" attitudes from parents and society or represent philosophies generated for economic and political reasons.

History of Racism

Before describing human origins and the causes of different human traits based on spontaneous natural genetic drift, i.e., changes in our DNA, the author thought that a brief history of racism would be appropriate. According to Fredrickson's book on "Racism, A Short History," (see Appendix III for full references). racism appears to have arisen in the early medieval times (11th and 12th centuries). However, the term racism came into common usage in the 1930s to describe the theories behind the Nazi's persecution of the Jews. Racism is deemed more than "xenophobia," a Greek term for distrust and hostility to strangers or foreigners. Rather, racism infers that those who are different cannot coexist or assimilate into the local society. People who were racially targeted were often thought as "less than human." Such philosophies were probably enhanced in the late middle ages by the nobility who believed in "noble blood" of their offspring, which conveniently maintained their position, power, and possessions.

The concept of race did not exist in the Greek or Roman era or even in the early Christian era. Slaves were of all skin shades, religions, and cultures. Slaves and non-Christians were able to convert their status to become Christians and be assimilated. However, an early example of racism is documented in the 10th - 14th centuries, with the hostility and even massacre, of the Jewish people in Europe. This hostility was generated by the attitude that the Jewish people could not convert or be assimilated and were intrinsically and physically evil [Fredrickson (2002) "Racism, A Short History"]. Bad events such as the Black Death and bad weather were often blamed on the Jewish people. Even those Muslims and Jews who converted to Christianity in 15th and 16th century Spain, were eventually deemed outcasts and evil by nature. This rise of "racism" eventually occurred all over Europe during this period.

In the 19th century Germany, the status of the Jewish people broadly ranged from acceptance to lesser status without full rights. As the Jewish people became prosperous, animosity and racist attitudes against them increased, and peaked in the 20th century. Many Germans blamed the Jews for the loss of World War I, the depressions, and an overall conspiracy to dominate German society and culture. Christian Germans were deemed spiritual and poetic, and derived from a superior race, while Jews were deemed materialistic, unscrupulous, and thought to possess impure blood. It is interesting that during the first quarter of the 20th century, up to 23% of the Jews were marrying non-Jews in Germany. This soon ended in the 1930s. It should be mentioned that most of Europe and the Americas engendered an anti-Semitic view as well, but probably not to the extreme it existed in Germany.

The Germans in the early 20th century South Africa attempted to exterminate the Herero tribe, as well as the NAMA tribe, for their lands. One wonders whether this mindset in South Africa set the stage for the later attempted annihilation of European Jewry via the concentration camps and the "Death Squads" in Western Russia in World War II. In his book, Racism, Fredrickson states that "the often overlooked pre-Nazi German genocide in South Africa shows that German racism and final solutions were not directed exclusively at the Jewish people."

In Medieval Europe, other ethnic groups such as the Irish, certain Slavic peoples, and others, whose behaviors resembled heresy to the main society, also became targets of racism. Interestingly, in the 16th -19th century, in areas of the world controlled by Spain, the American Indians and black Africans who accepted Christianity (and Spanish leadership) were generally not categorized as "lesser humans" and did not carry impure blood.

Europeans had little contact with dark skinned (sub-Saharan) Africans up to the 15th century. Africans enjoyed little racism and even acceptance in the medieval times. The

Europeans were the first to devise and support the concept of "Polygenesis" which held the view that different races, as well as classes of citizens (rich versus poor; nobility versus non-nobility), were very different and to such an unalterable magnitude, that they were deemed "lesser humans."

Beginning around the 15th century, Spain (and Europe) did accept Africans as slaves. They justified these actions based on a religious interpretation of the Bible's Book of Genesis. A general view arose that black Africans were cursed. Thus, the Muslims' introduction of Africans as slaves to Christian Spain was readily accepted on this religious basis. This philosophy carried over into antebellum United States to support that racial slavery was divinely sanctioned (let alone useful for plantation labor). Between the 17th century and 19th century, the slave trade in the United States, a country founded on equal rights of all people, was booming. White supremacy fully reigned in the U.S. between the 1890s and 1950s, and survived in South Africa until 1980.

In summary, the racism of the white supremacy era in the United States and the anti-Semitism in Europe originated during the late medieval era and continued and even increased up to the 20th century. Certain philosophies such as religious curses and polygenesis influenced and bolstered the pro-slavery leaders of European descent in the USA, a country founded on "all men created equal and endowed with individual rights." Extreme racial atrocities as genocide seem to occur when governments themselves take on racist views. In his book, "Racism: A Short History," Fredrickson describes the history of how racist governments combined with supportive or indifferent citizens, allow, or even encourage, extreme policies and measures to persecute or even eliminate the "targeted" ones. Racism is a hidden disease, and can infect a whole society or nation and ultimately destroy it.

Chapter 2

The Origins of Modern Humans

2

The Origins of Modern Humans

Definitions

Physical Anthropology: Study of mankind through their physical and cultural characteristics, their customs and social relationships, etc.

Archeology: Study of life and culture of the past, ancient peoples, relics, tools, architecture.

Generation: The time required for a newborn baby to mature to generate another baby. In this book a generation is assumed to be 20 years.

African Origins of All Humans

Physical Anthropologic findings have shown that all humans today (called Homo sapiens) originated in Eastern Africa in or near the region, known as the Rift Valley, 200,000 years ago

(10,000 generations ago) (see Appendix I, Note 3, for information on past ancient humans). Table 2.1 outlines some interesting dates of modern human history (Homo sapiens) along with the average number of past generations. The first evidence of modern humans (Homo sapiens) appears only 200,000 years ago (10,000 generations ago). Interestingly, these modern human ancestors spent approximately 70-75% of their existence (or approximately 150,000 years) migrating all over Africa, dating from approximately 200,000 years ago to 50,000 years ago.

There were periods approximately 140,000 to 70,000 years ago when the human population diminished in Africa due to periods of frigid ice ages, which created extreme arid conditions including desert lands, loss of habitat, and food scarcity. There is evidence that modern human adventurers did immigrate out of Africa into the Middle East approximately 100,000 to 80,000 years ago, but either perished there or retreated to Africa approximately 80,000 to 70,000 years ago, at a time of a major change in the global environment. This global environmental change has been blamed by some scientists on a massive volcanic eruption of Mount Tobol in Indonesia approximately 75,000 years ago. In summary, the newer genomic analyses in the new field of

Molecular Anthropology support those of Physical Anthropology and Archaeology findings, confirming that all modern humans originated in Africa. Thus, one could say "we are all African."

Exiting Africa

Around 60,000 to 50,000 years ago, modern humans permanently exited Africa, both to the Middle East and across Southern Arabia to India, and migrated to all parts of the earth. Table 2.1 goes on to identify that more permanent dwellings appeared approximately 20,000 years ago (1,000 generations ago), with farming and domestication of animals occurring after the last ice age, approximately 14,000 - 12,000 years ago (600 generations ago). In essence, our ancestors, about 1000 generations ago and before, were what we commonly refer to as "cave men," foraging for food as hunters-gatherers. The extent of their communication skills is not known, but is speculated to be very good involving the earliest forms of languages. Our ancestors 20,000 years ago were certainly capable of building shelters, using sophisticated tools, creating jewelry, and crossing large bodies of water. Recent archeological evidence in the Mediterranean indicates that humans may have crossed the sea to islands over 10,000 years ago. As listed in Table 2.1, only about 6,000 years ago (300 generations ago), humans began their first civilizations in Mesopotamia and Egypt.

Those that departed Africa did so as dark skinned Homo sapiens about 50,000 years ago (~2,500 generations ago) and they ended up in Europe/Asia as light skinned Eurasians thousands of years later. There were other physical and physiological (metabolic) changes as well, which will be discussed later. How did these changes in physical appearance and internal physiology happen? Was it something unique, a mysterious immediate event that caused this? The answer is "NO!"

As discussed in the next chapter, the physical and physiological changes in humans are now better understood via Molecular Anthropology and Molecular Genetics, as being due to spontaneous gradual changes in our genetic make-up (i.e., genetic drift). The following chapters summarize these processes to help promote an understanding of where we came from and who we are. In essence, our DNA defines who we really are, where we originated, and the migrations that our ancestors took to populate the earth.

Table 2.1

Overview: History of Modern Humans via Anthropology / Archeology

Event	Generations Ago (Each generation ≈ 20 yr)	Years Ago
Homo sapiens (modern man)	10,000	200,000
Migrations out of Africa	~2,500	50-60,000
Dwellings/Farming	500-1,000	~10-20,000
First Civilizations	300	6,000
Moses/Christ	100-175	2-3,500

Table 2.1 List of important events in the history of modern humans via anthropology and archeology.

Chapter 3

The Human Genome: The Genetic Material that Makes Us Who We Are

3

The Human Genome: The Genetic Material that Makes Us Who We Are

Definitions

Human Genome: Taken from the Greek language, refers to all the DNA (genes) in all the chromosomes of an organism. In humans, this consists of the DNA in all 23 pairs of chromosomes in the cell nucleus, as well as DNA in a cell organelle called the mitochondria (see definition below).

Human Genome Project: The complete analysis of human DNA (genetic information) that required 10 years and 3 billion dollars to complete. The project involved the sequencing (determining the order) of 3 billion bits of information along the DNA.

DNA (Deoxyribonucleic Acid): The genetic material found in the cell nucleus carries the genetic information as "genes." It consists of two thin threads of sugars (polysaccharides) bound to each other side by side via pairing of bases (base pairs) which are bound to the sugars.

Bases and base pairs: Bases are the four chemical compounds abbreviated (A, T, G, and C) which, in a series, carry the genetic information which determines human physical appearance and metabolism. These are the letters in the language of life. These bases, in a long series, contain the genetic information that the cell uses in groups called "genes." The cell uses this genetic information to assemble proteins to create and maintain each human body. Bases are bound as pairs (G-C and A-T) in the double-stranded DNA molecule and serve as genetic markers in genetics.

Chromosome: Thread-like structure found in the nuclei of most living cells consisting of multi-folded/compacted DNA strands carrying the genetic information as DNA (genes).

Gene: A distinct sequence (region) of DNA found in chromosomes, whose base sequence codes for proteins which, in turn, determine the traits/properties of a human being. Humans have a total of 20,000 to 25,000 genes which are inherited, i.e., passed on to subsequent generations.

DNA sequencing: A laboratory technique for determining the exact sequence, i.e., order of occurrence, of the 4 known bases that are abbreviated by the letters G, C, A, and T.

Mutation: A rare, spontaneous change in the sequence of bases which is passed on to subsequent generations. This usually occurs in <.001% of the population. During cell replication, the DNA is replicated and passed on to the daughter cell. Mutations are errors created in the DNA during DNA replication, which are also passed on with the rest of the DNA to future generations. The process occurs spontaneously, and ultimately causes "Genetic Drift" in populations. The process occurs in one or a few individuals and can expand in frequency in a population to become a polymorphism.

Polymorphism: A term used when mutations increase in numbers to approximately 1% or more of the population. As the population expands, changes in polymorphisms (base sequence changes) often create changes in human traits. These changes occur spontaneously and periodically and their appearance can be roughly dated. This process represents the foundations of "Genetic Drift" in populations.

(See Appendix I, Notes 1 and 2, for additional details.)

X chromosome: One of two sex chromosomes containing genes which determine the gender of an individual. Two X chromosomes, each donated from the father and mother, create a female. One X chromosome from the mother and one Y chromosome from the father create a male.

Y chromosome: One of the two sex chromosomes containing genes which determine the gender of an individual. Inherited only from the father (male inheritance). Used to trace male (father) lineages. The male (carrying an X and a Y) thus determines the sex of any offspring by donating either an X or a Y to the mother's X chromosome during fertilization of the egg (see Figure 4.1).

Mitochondria: Energy producing bodies in all human cells which contain their own DNA packaged as a small chromosome. All mitochondria and their DNA are inherited only from the mother (female inheritance), so both the boys and girls inherit the mother's mitochondrial DNA. However, only the girls pass on their particular mitochondrial DNA to subsequent generations. Thus, this mitochondrial DNA and its polymorphisms are used to trace female lineages (see Figure 4.1) (see Appendix 1, Note 7, for added information).

Note: See Appendix I, Notes 1 and 2, for more detailed description/definitions of important genetic terminology.

The Human Genome, the Human Genome Project, and DNA Polymorphisms

There is a common genetic link among all humans and among all life. The term "human genome" refers to all the DNA in all the chromosomes of any human. The total chromosomal DNA (i.e., the genome) contains the genetic information (genes) that codes for each human. The term "human genome" became popular with the achievement of the Human Genome project which involved the DNA sequencing of the entire human genome, i.e., all the DNA in all the chromosomes. (See Appendix 1, Notes 1 and 2 for further details.)

Spontaneous changes in the human genome, called mutations, occur periodically and spontaneously in the human genome through a process called "Genetic Drift." Sometimes these mutations expand in a population to become polymorphisms. These polymorphisms (referred to as changes in genetic markers from the original populations) serve to create the physical and metabolic differences among various ethnic groups and even among individual humans on the earth. Since the mutations and subsequent polymorphisms occur at a relatively constant frequency, the patterns of these polymorphisms allow estimations of approximate dates of these events as well as the genetic tracking of human origins and world migrations.

Each cell in our body has 46 chromosomes, which occur in pairs, 23 from the father's sperm and 23 from the mother's egg. Two of these 46 pairs represent the sex chromosomes. In males, the X chromosome is donated by the mother and the Y chromosome is donated by the father, and, in females, there are two X chromosomes (one each donated by the father and mother). Thus, it is the father's sperm, carrying one Y or one X chromosome, which determines the sex of the embryo upon fertilization.

Organisms of the same species have the same size, organization, and number of chromosomes and, thus, can produce fertile offspring via egg and sperm. Organisms of different species have different types, organization, and/or number of chromosomes and thus cannot create a viable embryo or at least cannot produce fertile offspring. To create a human embryo, and ultimately a baby, after fertilization of the sperm and egg, each of the same classes of 23 chromosomes from the sperm and those from the egg join as pairs to create the initial embryonic cell with the required 46 chromosomes for a living cell. This cell then replicates its DNA and divides into 2 cells, then 2 cells into 4, 4 into 8, and so on to create a human with 10 trillion (10×10^{12}) cells. Thus, each cell in an adult human contains the same 46 chromosomes. However, as cells divide, they begin to differ from one another early on during embryo development to become 200 different types of cells which make up tissues and organs of the adult human. This is achieved by varying the activities of the genes from one cell type to another.

Our DNA, and that of all living organisms, has some remarkable physical features. The DNA is located in our chromosomes as depicted in Figure 3.1. As depicted in Table 3.1, each chromosome has one long double strand of DNA which is about 3 to 4 inches of unwound DNA threads. In each of our cells, the 46 chromosomes combine to make 12 feet of double-stranded DNA end to end.

It is hard to imagine that the total DNA in the 10 trillion (10^{13}) cells in the human body stretches approximately 24 billion miles

Figure 3.1

The Human Genome and Genome Project
The Human Genome Information would fill 200 city phone books or 2000 average computer diskettes

Cell — Nucleus

Chromosome (Unraveling)

The Human Genome Project sequenced all the DNA in all the chromosomes

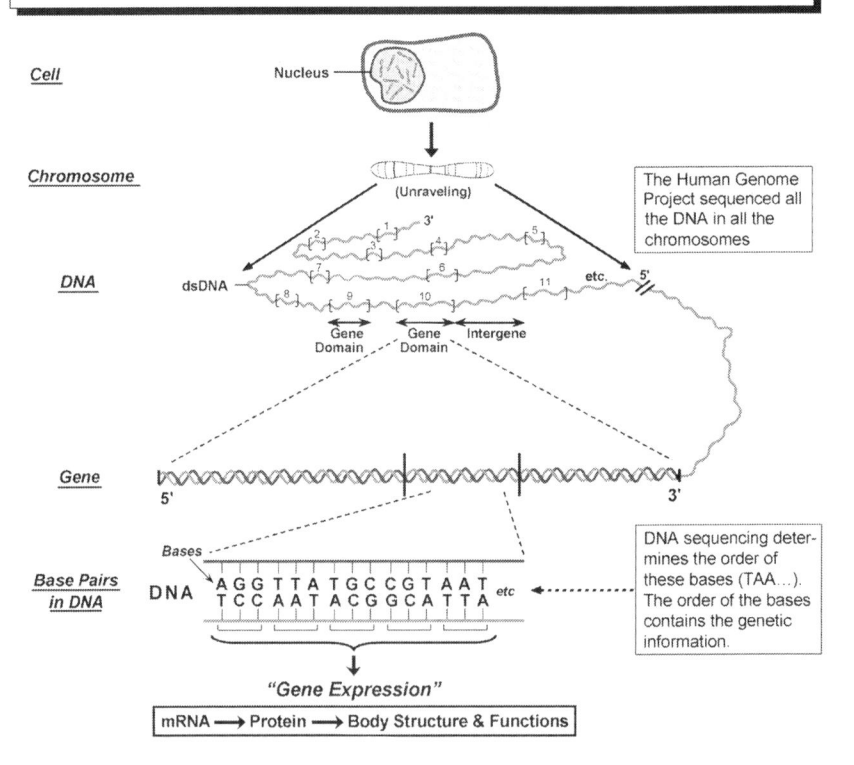

DNA — dsDNA — 3' ... 5'
Gene Domain | Gene Domain | Intergene

Gene 5' ———— 3'

Base Pairs in DNA — DNA
A G G T T A T G C C G T A A T etc
T C C A A T A C G G C A T T A

DNA sequencing determines the order of these bases (TAA...). The order of the bases contains the genetic information.

↓
"Gene Expression"
mRNA ⟶ Protein ⟶ Body Structure & Functions

Figure 3.1 Model of human genome structure from cell nuclei to chromosomes, to double stranded DNA with base pairings.

Table 3.1

Complexity of the Human Body

Entity	Number
Types of Cells/Body:	≈ 200
Cells/Body:	10 Trillion (10^{13})
DNA (length)/Cell:	12 feet
DNA (width):	2×10^{-9} meters
Ratio of DNA Length/Width:	40 Million to 1 per chromosome or 2 Billion to 1 per cell
Total DNA Length/Body:	24 Billion miles (24×10^9 miles)
Genes/Cell:	20,000 – 25,000
Molecules/Cell(incl. water):	≈ 10-100 Trillion (10^{13}-10^{14} molecules)
Molecules/Body:	10^{28} (1 followed by 28 zeros)
Chemical Rx/Cell/Min:	Billions

Table 3.1 Complexity of the human body.

(that's approximately 260 times the distance between the sun and earth). The thousands-fold compaction of this DNA into chromosomes is possible only because in each chromosome, the DNA thread is 40 million times longer than it is wide. To give a better perspective, if the width of a DNA strand is enlarged to about ¼ of an inch (about as wide as a pencil), the length of the DNA in each chromosome would stretch to approximately 4,000 miles, a distance longer than the distance between New York and Los Angeles.

The structure of the DNA molecule itself is intriguing. The DNA in a chromosome actually contains 2 threads of DNA, each as a chain of sugar molecules, with each sugar having an attached chemical structure called a base. The bases on one thread are bound to those on the other parallel thread to create a double-stranded (threaded) DNA. These bound bases are referred to simply as base pairs. In certain locations along the DNA, the sequence (i.e., the order in which they occur) of the bases on each thread contains genetic information as depicted in Figure 3.1.

For the human genome project, the DNA in all of the chromosomes (the genome), was sequenced to determine the order of the bases along the DNA strand. The sequencing of the DNA for the Human Genome Project followed these steps: 1) The DNA strands (one per chromosome) were unraveled. 2) The bases along the strand were then sequenced, in order, along the DNA strand and the information was stored in computer banks. (In all, there are three billion bases.) 3) Finally, the sequenced data were stored and analyzed by computer programs. This amazing feat took 3 billion dollars and 10 years to achieve. Improved techniques in DNA sequencing, instrumentation, and computer technology were required to achieve this feat.

Since then, the further improvements in sequencing have made the sequencing of genomes of humans, and that of many other living organisms, faster and cheaper. Today, the sequencing of the whole human genome can be achieved using less than $10,000.00 and can be completed in days. Thousands of humans have had their DNA wholly or partially sequenced and hundreds have had their genome fully sequenced. The goal of geneticists and the molecular medicine field is to have a $1,000 full genomic analysis available to every human.

Characterizing the Human Genome

Many interesting discoveries have been achieved regarding the genomes of humans and other animal, plant, and microbial species. One of the amazing discoveries from the Human Genome Project is the fact that only 1-2% of the whole genome has "functional genes" (i.e., regions coding for proteins that often determine traits) (see Appendix I, Note 2, for more details). Only half of these functional genes have been identified with specific functions, i.e., what they do.

Another discovery is the similarity of the gene sequences among all living organisms from humans, to monkeys, plants, and even bacteria. It has been known for many years that the genetic information (i.e., the "genetic code" in the DNA) is very similar among all living things on earth. Now we know that many genes have similar sequences among different species of life on earth. As an example, Figure 3.2 shows the segment of a typical gene, myoglobin, from both a human and a whale. The indicated differences in the gene from humans and whales could be classified as polymorphisms (differences in the order of base sequence). The observed similarities in the sequences of bases between the two are remarkable. When one extends these

Figure 3.2

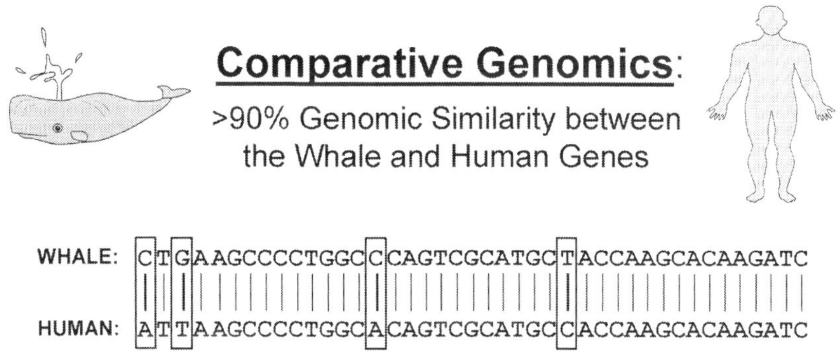

Comparative Genomics:
\>90% Genomic Similarity between the Whale and Human Genes

WHALE: CTGAAGCCCCTGGCCCAGTCGCATGCTACCAAGCACAAGATC

analyses to all genes of other organisms, even more amazing similarities are found. Figure 3.3 shows the gene sequence similarities of humans to other living organisms such as monkeys, mice, plants, insects, and microbes (bacteria).

Another amazing discovery of the Human Genome Project, shown in Figure 3.3, is the percent of genes in other living creatures which are similar to those of humans. The 98% similarity with primates is shockingly similar, yet not that hard to believe. However, it is harder for one to accept that 90% of the genes in rats, mice, dogs, cows, and other mammals are similar to humans. I guess the statements in the 1940s gangster movies of "You dirty rat" were not too far off, at least for the rat part. Even plants, worms, yeast, and bacterial genes share significant gene similarities with humans.

What, to the author, is so pleasing about these gene or genomic similarities is the realization that there is a strong genetic link among all life on Earth. What is the rationale for this significant gene similarity among all living things? It is simply that the functions of most of our genes are to carry out basic life processes such as cell replication, cell synthesis of needed cell components, cell repair, energy production, respiration, and

Figure 3.3

Comparative Genomics
(Genome Similarities Among Living Organisms)

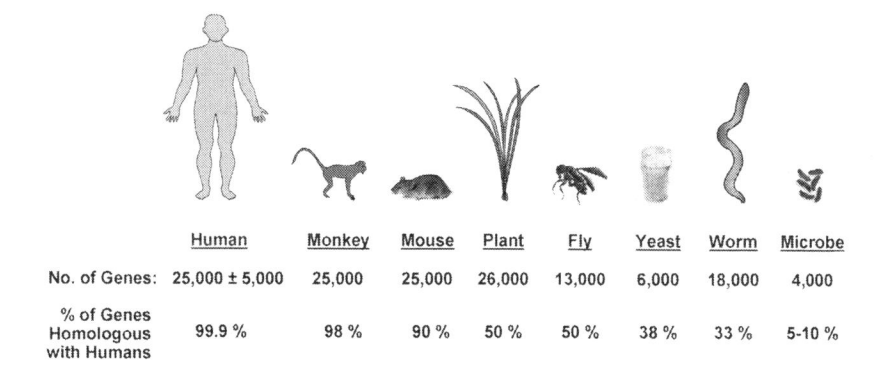

	Human	Monkey	Mouse	Plant	Fly	Yeast	Worm	Microbe
No. of Genes:	25,000 ± 5,000	25,000	25,000	26,000	13,000	6,000	18,000	4,000
% of Genes Homologous with Humans	99.9 %	98 %	90 %	50 %	50 %	38 %	33 %	5-10 %

Figure 3.3 Comparative genomics of living organisms, including gene number and gene homologies compared to the human genome.

metabolism. At this fundamental level, all life is the same or at least similar. Thus, the strong genetic similarities among living organisms are due to the fact that many genes are involved in the same basic life functions. Thus, all life is related; all life is precious. On a more practical note, the significant similarity in gene sequences between humans (99.9%) and mammal species (90%) has benefits as it has fostered the use of other animals as models to assess the roles of genes in causing diseases. Scientists can create human diseases in rodents by disturbing the same genes that are affected in human diseases.

What is also amazing is the fact that, referring back to Table 3.1, the human body is extremely complex. There are, in each of us, ten trillion cells (10×10^{12} cells) which are specialized into 200 different types. Each cell has trillions of molecules and millions of chemical reactions occurring every minute. It is also fascinating that all these cells and their molecules act in a coordinated pattern with each other to maintain life. How could all this complexity arise from only 20,000 - 25,000 genes? This discrepancy can be explained by the fact that each gene often codes for multiple products (proteins), and these protein products function in various combinations with each other. These added complexities of our genes lead to millions of possibilities and thus, certainly can account for the complexity of the human body.

Chapter 4

Using Polymorphisms to Track Human Origins and World Migrations

4

Using Polymorphisms to Track Human Origins and World Migrations

Definitions

Haplotype: The individual pattern of genetic markers (polymorphisms) found in the DNA of individual humans which categorizes them with other humans, as related to family members. Some represent more recently created markers used to identify recent relatives. Thus, individuals with the same haplotype are closely related and the more different the haplotype, the more distantly they are related. These haplotype patterns are located on either the male Y chromosomal DNA, or the female mitochondrial DNA.

Haplogroups: A large group of people who share the same vast, but unique, polymorphism patterns. Each group contains several to many related haplotypes and are used to define branches of the tree depicting early human origins and ancestry.

Using Polymorphisms to Track Human Migrations

Genetic markers can be (and are) used to track humans, their origins, and migrations worldwide. Some patterns of genetic markers can be used to decipher between more recent lineages and migrations while others are used to identify more ancient lineages and ancient migrations. (See Appendix I, Note 6, Figure 3, for further details.) These patterns are used to trace the origins and migrations of the male (father), when located in the Y chromosomal DNA, or the female (mother), when located in the mitochondrial DNA. (See Appendix I, Note 7, for further details about mitochondria.)

Note: The technical process/details about genetic markers (DNA polymorphisms), how they form, and the various classes of polymorphisms, are introduced in Chapter 3, but described in more detail in Appendix II at the end of this book.

As described in Appendices I and II, and Chapter 3, these genetic markers (DNA polymorphisms) begin as rare mutations.

When they occur in 1% of the individuals in a population, they are reclassified as polymorphisms. Figure 4.1 shows an example of a mutation/polymorphism shown as a single change in base sequence. These changes begin early in embryos, as demonstrated by the fact that identical twins who evolve from one fertilized egg will, even at birth, display a slightly different pattern of polymorphisms. Identical twins will gradually differ in appearance more and more as they age, since the patterns of polymorphisms continue to differ more and more.

Also depicted in Figure 4.1, our DNA is found both in the nucleus as 46 total chromosomes (left side) and in our mitochondria (right side of Figure). Shown on the lower left side of Figure 4.1, the analysis of the genetic markers (polymorphisms) in the Y chromosome, found in the cell nucleus as one of the 46 chromosomes, can be used to identify "male only" heritage as only the males contribute this Y chromosome to their male descendants. Alternately, assessing genetic markers (DNA polymorphisms) in the DNA of mitochondria, an organelle found outside the nucleus in the cell cytoplasm (lower right side of Figure 4.1), permits analyses of "female only" heritage as only the females contribute the mitochondria to their descendants.

Figure 4.1

Analyzing Human Genomes for Ancestry and Disease Predisposition

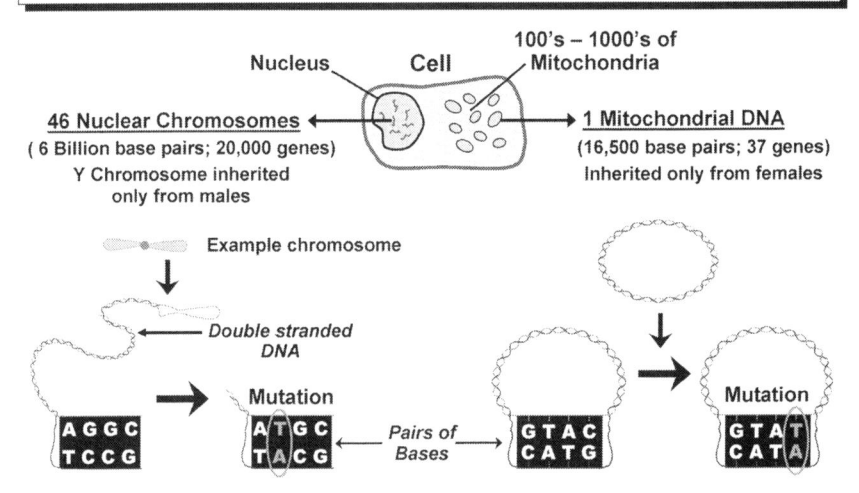

100's – 1000's of Mitochondria
Nucleus
Cell

46 Nuclear Chromosomes
(6 Billion base pairs; 20,000 genes)
Y Chromosome inherited only from males

1 Mitochondrial DNA
(16,500 base pairs; 37 genes)
Inherited only from females

Example chromosome

Double stranded DNA

Mutation

AGGC → ATGC ← Pairs of → GTAC → GTAT
TCCG   TACG   Bases   CATG   CATA

Mutation

Single nucleotide polymorphisms represent 95% of the total polymorphisms
5% of DNA polymorphisms represent insertions or deletions of larger DNA segments (multi bases).

Figure 4.1 Model outlining the analysis of the human genome for ancestry and disease predisposition.

Scientists use the patterns of multiple polymorphisms from these two sources to identify each of us as individuals, our relatives, and our ancestry. It should be noted that the 0.1% genetic difference among all humans on the earth represents about three million base differences between individuals (0.1% of the three billion total bases). Interestingly, only a fraction of these, 1 out of 10 or even 1 out of 30 base changes (i.e. polymorphisms), are actually involved in causing all humans to be different. The remaining differences have no known biological effect on human differences. Thus, about 0.003% to 0.01% (or a change of 1 out of 100,000 bases) in our genome actually make us different from each other. This represents approximately 30,000 base differences in individual whole genomes made up of three billion bases.

Since it is known that these markers are created at fairly consistent frequencies in the genome (see Appendix II for details), the changes in genetic markers (in the DNA) can be used not only to retrace the ancestors' ancient locations, but also the estimated dates of these locations. Each genome actually contains a pattern of many polymorphisms, called haplotypes, which enable molecular anthropologists to compare populations to each other, as well as one individual to another, and to more accurately trace and date origins of human lineages.

How are these genetic markers used to track our ancestry? As shown in the model in Figure 4.2, going from left to right, an original population (group 1) in location 1, migrates 30,000 years ago (YA) to location 2 which later obtained a change in bases A-T to G-C. Then sometime later, a branch "group 2" migrates from location 2 to location 3, wherein another set of bases are changed (T-A to C-G). Another, "group 5," migrates from location 2 to location 6, with a change of G-C to A-T. Later, about 10,000 years ago, "groups 3 and 4" migrate to locations 4 and 5, wherein base changes again occur. Such migrations and changes continue on for many locations throughout the world. Each group resides in one geographic location for an extended period before a group of its members moves on, carrying with them the markers of that population. During these extended periods at each location, specific polymorphisms spontaneously arise in the population in that location and continue to expand into large numbers in that population over thousands of years. Since polymorphisms appear at relatively constant periodic intervals, the ages of these human migrations can also be estimated.

Figure 4.2

Using Polymorphisms to Trace Human Migrations

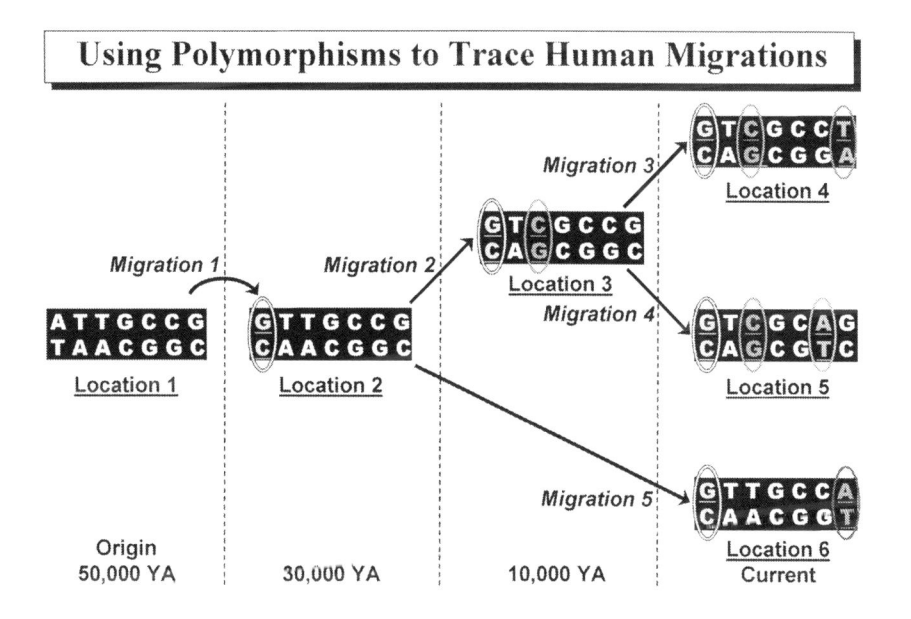

Figure 4.2 Model using DNA polymorphisms to trace human migrations.

Using this analysis of the Y chromosome and mitochondrial chromosome, together with computer analysis of a multitude of genetic markers at various geographic locations, one can retrace the origins of the current populations in all locations, in chronological order (by age). Locations 4 and 5 (Figure 4.2) would be logical offshoots of location 3. Location 3 would be an obvious offshoot of location 2. Location 6 would be the offshoot of location 2. The true origin of all groups would be the peoples of location 1. Using analyses from the biological samples obtained from thousands of individuals throughout the world, Molecular Anthropologists are tracking our ancestors back in time and to various locations.

Sampling Our DNA

What are the human biological samples from which the DNA is extracted and analyzed and how are they obtained? Modern day technology has made it all much easier. As outlined in Figure 4.3, the DNA samples of individuals from around the world are obtained from their blood cells, cheek swabs, or saliva. Specific regions of the DNA are then amplified thousands of fold by using a laboratory technique called PCR or polymerase chain reaction,

Figure 4.3

How Individual Genomic Polymorphisms are Obtained

Lab
Cheek swab, blood, or saliva
↓
Isolated cells from individual
↓
DNA (genome) of individual
↓
Polymerase chain amplification (Polymerase chain reaction)
↓
Sequencing of specific regions of DNA
↓

Computer Analyses
Data entered into computer and analyzed
↓
Comparison of base sequences
↓
Indentification of polymorphisms
↓
Computation of past geographic locations (i.e., migrations) at different times
↓
How you got where you are today

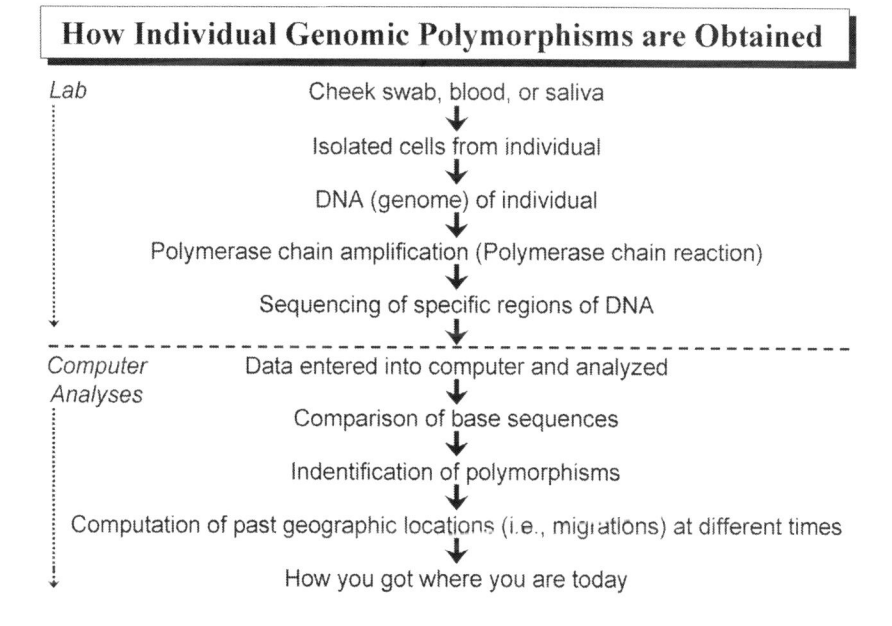

Figure 4.3 Chart outlining how biological samples for individual genomic polymorphisms are obtained.

and specific regions of this amplified DNA are sequenced. The base sequences A-G; G-C; T-A, etc., are fed into computers for comparative analysis, and for the identification of differences in genetic markers. Molecular Anthropologists use these patterns of genetic markers to decipher approximate origins and migration routes, together with rough timelines of many populations on all continents. Currently there are various commercial entities (see Appendix V) which offer to trace one's ancestry - recent or remote.

Populating the Earth

Figure 4.4 is a map representing the summation of modern man's early migrations out of Africa to inhabit the earth. As depicted in Panel A (Figure 4.4), molecular anthropology has shown that modern humans (Homo sapiens), appeared in Africa approximately 200,000 years ago (YA), and their offspring spent approximately 150,000 years migrating around and populating the African continent. Then, possibly due to a changing climate with the resulting food limitations, or even curiosity and desire for "new/better things," some of our early ancestors permanently migrated out of Africa, 60,000 to 50,000 years ago. Those

Figure 4.4

Earliest Modern Human Migrations Out of Africa via Genetics

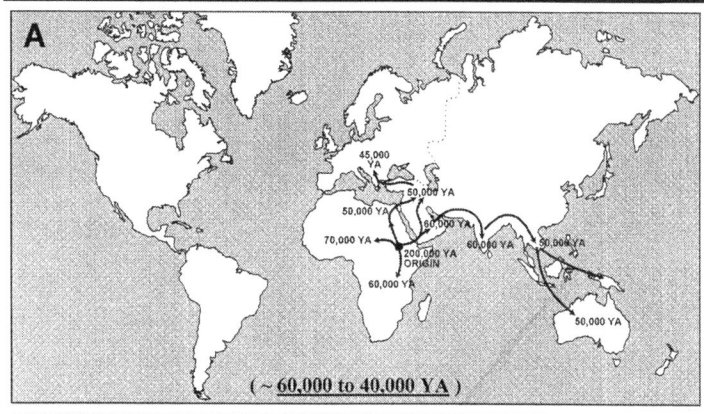

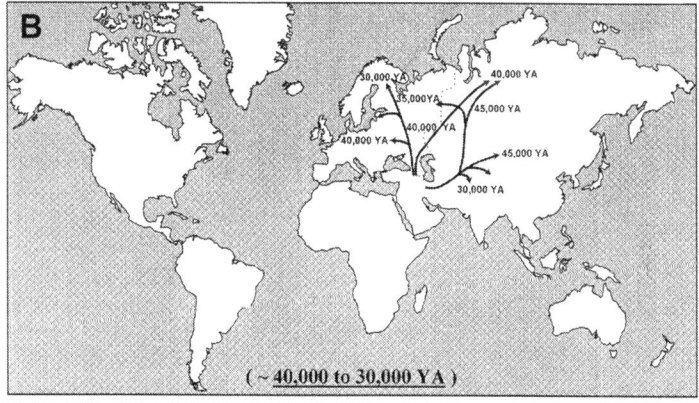

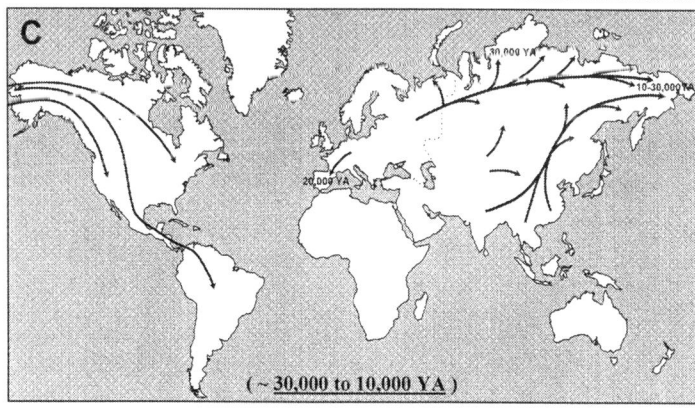

A (~ 60,000 to 40,000 YA)

B (~ 40,000 to 30,000 YA)

C (~ 30,000 to 10,000 YA)

Figure 4.4 World map depicting the time periods and migration routes of modern humans out of Africa and around the world 60,000 to 10,000 YA (years ago).(Data taken from Spencer Wells, 2006, Deep Ancestry: Inside the Genographic Project, Natl Geo.)

---

remaining in Africa migrated all over the African continent for similar reasons.

Anthropologic data also indicate that first modern humans had minor excursions out of Africa as early as 100,000 - 90,000 years ago, into the Middle East, only to disappear or withdraw back to Africa approximately 70,000 years ago. Climatic changes probably caused this disappearance as the whole African human population declined and almost became extinct at that time. However, later migrations out of Africa about 60,000 to 50,000 years ago were permanent. Major wave after major wave occurred out of Africa at different places and times over the period of 50,000 to 10,000 years ago. Panels B and C of Figure 4.4 show the continuation of migrations throughout the world. Many Archeological and Physical Anthropological data support these routes.

It should be pointed out that these maps represent major migration routes and are simplifications of the actual multitude of continuous migrations occurring throughout the 50,000 to 10,000 years ago period. The migration arrows only show the general direction. What is not depicted are people settling down in each region along the indicated migratory arrows, as well as the many offshoots from these major arrows, i.e., secondary migrations from the major migrations. Also not depicted are some groups reversing direction or making large migrating loops which cross connect with old routes. The causes of the multiple sub-migrations are unknown, but are probably based on food sources (animal migrations), etc. In any case, these genetic ancestry maps (Figure 4.4 and 4.5) do give us a general idea of human origins and early migrations.

Populating the Middle East and Europe

As emphasized above, the complexity of human migrations and the co-mixing of various groups of humans across the world is further exemplified by the more thorough studies of the more recent major migrations in Europe and Middle East around 20,000 – 10,000 years ago. As depicted in Figures 4.5 and 4.6, subsequent major migrations occurred from Asia and the Middle East to Europe during 30,000 to 10,000 years ago with additional

Figure 4.5

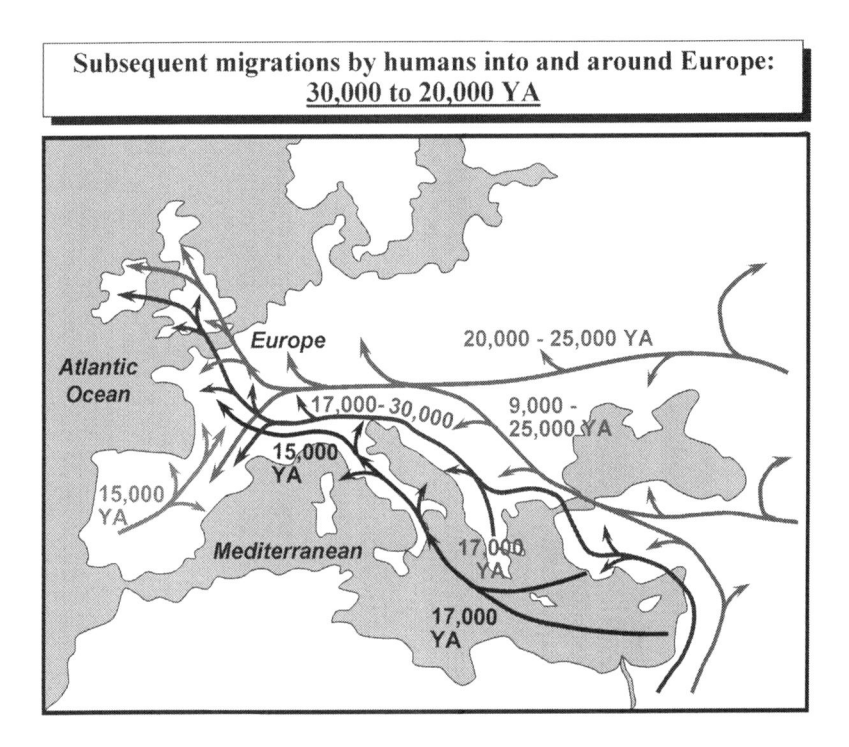

Figure 4.5 Subsequent migrations by humans into and around Europe (30,000 to 20,000 YA). (Data taken from S. Molenyak and Turner 2004, "Trace Your Roots with DNA", Rodale Pub.)

migrations from Africa through Spain to Europe. The subsequent migrating groups of people co-mixed with earlier tribes/communities that had previously settled in Europe. According to Wells (2006) and other sources (see Appendix III), and as depicted in Figure 4.6, even further major co-mixing of peoples occurred at the beginning of the last ice age (approximately 25,000 years ago), whereby all the peoples of Northern Europe migrated to the middle to southern parts of Europe to escape the cold and glaciers. Further co-mixing occurred as a result of a "reverse" migration, whereby some of these southern populations returned to Northern Europe after the last ice age ending approximately 12,000 years ago).

Figure 4.6

Return migrations <u>after 10,000</u> BC by humans who had taken refuge in warmer climates during the previous Ice Age

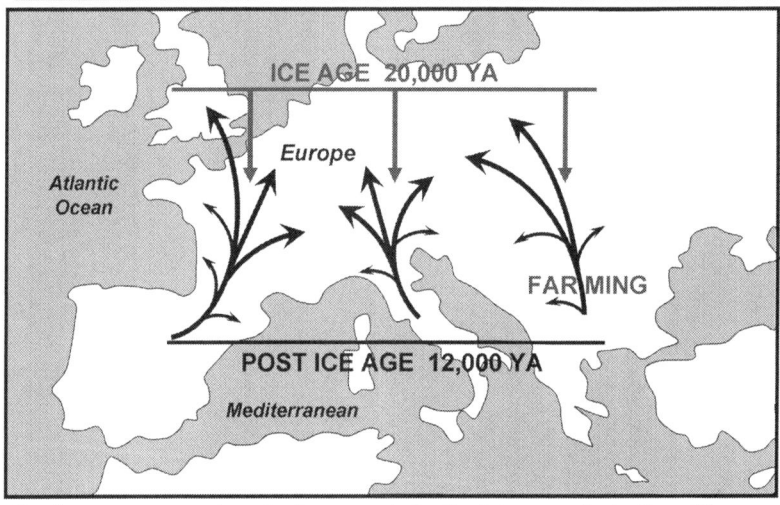

ICE AGE 20,000 YA
Europe
Atlantic Ocean
FARMING
POST ICE AGE 12,000 YA
Mediterranean

Southern areas served as staging grounds for the future recolonization of Europe.

<u>Figure 4.6</u> European/Asian map of human migrations before and after the last Ice Age (25,000 to 12,000 YA). (Data taken from Spencer Wells, 2006, Deep Ancestry: Inside the Genographic Project, Natl Geo.)

It is speculated that mankind migrated to various locations around the world in search of food, such as herds of wildlife, to escape harsh weather, for safety, over disputes among the group, or the desire for a better life. During this period, the discovery of farming and domestication of farm animals occurred in the Middle East (14,000 to 10,000 years ago) and elsewhere in Asia and the Americas. Subsequent human migrations brought farming to Western Asia and Europe.

Genomic studies of the male lineage (Y chromosome DNA) and female lineage (mitochondrial DNA) have indicated that the male farmers, migrating from the Middle East, mated primarily with the local females already residing in Europe. They could provide food and an easier, more stable lifestyle. Later, the indigenous male hunter/gatherers in the area eventually would also adopt this easier, more stable, lifestyle of farming and animal domestication.

What is the final outcome of all these primary, secondary, etc., migrations and co-mixing of populations? In Table 4.1, Sykes lists the tribal origins of the average European woman from his book, "The Seven Daughters of Eve" (see reference in Appendix III). There are at least 7 major lineages or tribes which have contributed genetic information to the typical European

Table 4.1

	Major Ancestral Origins of the Average European Females Living Today as Traced through the Mitochondrial DNA		
	TIME	ORIGINS	Population/Group
1.	45,000 YA	Greece	Ursula U
2.	25,000 YA	Middle East & Russia (Spread into Americas)	Xenia X
3.	20,000 YA	Border France & Spain Came from Middle East?	Helena H
4.	17,000 YA	Mediterranean	Tara T
5.	15,000 YA	Northern Italy	Katherine K
6.	15,000 YA	Spain/Portugal	Velda V
7.	9,000 YA	Mid-East with spread of Agriculture	Jasmine J

Table 4.1 Tribal/Population lineages of an average European woman. (YA = Years Ago); (Data taken from B. Sykes, 2001, Seven Daughters of Eve, WW Norton Co., NY).

woman. Similarly, there are also 7-10 different tribal lineages, some different from the female lineages, which comprise the average European male. These origins, of course, occurred after early humans migrated out of Africa. The overall message here is that there is no genetic "purity" in any European and no "purity" of race. Those of European decent are genetic mixtures of many different tribes. Similarly, those from Africa, Asia, and Australia have multiple tribal lineages. One might say peoples of Europe, and other continents for that matter, are genetic mongrels. In summary, we are now learning about the migrations of our ancestors, who are our cousins at one level or another, and how our ancestors migrated to all continents on the planet. (See Appendix I, Note 3, for additional information.)

Populating Asia and the Americas

Figures 4.4 and 4.5 also summarize the major migrations to Asia and the Americas. The North American Indian tribes often had genetic as well as cultural and language differences from each other. There appear to have been three major migrations into the Americas at different periods (25,000 - 8,000 years ago) with multiple smaller ones in between. Genomic analyses and anthropology suggest that some of these migrations (of Preclovis people) occurred before 20,000 years ago, well before the earliest evidence of Clovis people (approximately 13,000 years ago).

While all North American Indians share Asian genetic signatures, some carry genetic signatures (markers) originating from different specific regions of Southern vs Northern Asia. Some American Indian tribes share genetic markers with Europeans, (now found only in Druse, Italian, and Finish populations) from when their tribes separated long ago (approximately 30,000 - 20,000 years ago).

It has been speculated that the early American Indian migrants, which had genetic links to the European immigrants, had more European features. Later immigrants to the Americas (after 12,000 years ago) had more Mongolian features. Interestingly, the Mongolian/Asian features are now believed to have arisen during the last ice age (approximately 20,000 to 12,000 years ago), and were features of immigrants to the Americas arriving after that time.

Some Interesting Facts Revealed by Molecular Anthropology

1) Many facts have been generated from these genetic analyses which support the biblical history of the Old Testament. For example, the closest relatives of the Jewish populations, no matter where they reside around the world, have now been genetically linked to people who reside in current Middle Eastern populations, including Jordan, Syria, Palestine, and Arabs of the Saudi Arabian peninsula. This is interesting when one considers the conflict ongoing in that area. This relationship is due to the "not so ancient" origins of the Jewish people from the Middle East (3,200 to 2,000 years ago), as described in many religious texts. Overall, it is interesting to note that some Anthropologists state that, due to intermarriages outside all religious cultures, it is difficult to assign specific genetic signatures/markers to any one religion, whether Jewish, Muslim, Hindu, Buddhist, Catholic, Protestant, etc.

2) The genetic signatures of Macedonian/Grecian peoples are found in peoples in lands involving Alexander the Great's invasions of Egypt, the Middle East and Southern Asia (approximately 300 BC). The same goes for the subsequent genetic signatures in populations over most of Europe

approximately 450 AD, following the invasion of Attila the Hun from the Caspian Sea area, and the Mongolian genetic signatures in populations who experienced Genghis Khan's invasions (approximately 1215 AD). Surely similar signatures exist from other major invasions such as the Romans.

3) Some of the present day direct descendants of the 8,000 year old frozen ice man hunter from the Italian Alps have been identified from DNA data banks of people living today. The patterns of polymorphisms of currently living people whose genetic information was stored in the computer data banks were compared to the DNA still preserved in the bone marrow/tissue of the frozen ice man.

4) Present day direct descendants of Thomas Jefferson have been identified, some offspring were children of the African American slave, Sally Hemings, for whom Jefferson cared and whose children he freed.

5) The author had his genetic ancestry analyzed by Genographics, Inc. (of the National Geographic Society) and "23 and Me" companies. Using the family history and name, the author's father, born in Germany near Hagen, with the original "family" originating from the Remscheid area, actually had most of

his currently living genetic "cousins" in Ireland, with lesser numbers in the Basque region of Northern Spain, as well as Southern France and England. This is a common ancestry of many Irish men and follows a major route of migrations from Western Asia to Europe with the migrations ending in England and Ireland (see Figure 4.5).

The author's mother's ancestry, whose ancestors migrated to North America from Scotland and England, respectively (approximately 1600-1700s), has the highest frequency of living genetic cousins in the European Ashkenazi Jewish population with lesser lineages to the Druse in Syria/Jordan area in the Middle East, and Asian Kurds. This was learned via analyses of the author's sister's mitochondrial DNA. This information explains the author's mother's darker skin tone about which her children had always questioned. She was a mix of many cultures, as are all other European women and men.

6) The family history of the author's spouse, Liza, identifies an Irish ancestry. However, her genetics trace her ancient lineage out of Africa, straight through Europe to Scandinavia, 40,000 to 35,000 years ago. She has a very ancient European lineage, as do many European women. When she asked the author how her

ancestors more recently ended up in Ireland, after pondering a moment the author unwisely replied, "Liza, I think your ancestors may have been raping, pillaging Vikings." Obviously, that did not go over well. Actually, many Vikings migrated peacefully and settled in the British Isles and Ireland during the 700 to 1,200 AD period.

Chapter 5

Why and How Populations Become Different: The Role of Isolation and Environment

5

Why and How Populations Become Different: The Role of Isolation and Environment

Definitions

<u>Physical traits</u>: Visible features like eye color, hair structure, nose shape, and other features which are determined by inherited genes from our parents.

<u>Physiological/metabolic traits</u>: Invisible features relating to the physiology and metabolism/chemistry of an individual, including disease predispositions, which are also determined by inherited genes from our parents.

The Role of Environmental Selection

The biological/genetic rationale for genetic drift is to allow humans, and all living things, to adapt over time to new environments. (Appendix II describes this in more detail.) Without this ability to adapt, living organisms would more readily become extinct. This genetic drift has given all living organisms the critical ability for change (adaptation) during earth's climate changes and through migrations to different geographic locations and environments. The environment also enhances the rapidity of this change/adaptation due to selection of the fittest to survive. The rate of genetic drift is more profound as a result of human migrations because it creates rapid and extreme changes in the environment and ecology. Genetic drift also occurs more rapidly in small populations.

As described earlier, and in Appendix II, the changes in the environment will select the "best fit" individuals to survive and reproduce. Given enough time, and if the environment dictates such changes, our individual or population-wide physical traits can (and will) change and can even reverse if the environment is altered appropriately. The required time for the development of a trait in a population is shortened when strong environmental selection exists which favors certain traits over others. The fate of a mutation/polymorphism in a population, which creates a certain trait, depends on how it affects our bodies. Since certain traits are positive selectors (i.e., have an advantage over others in survival and reproducing offspring), individuals with these traits will gain over others in numbers and predominate in a population over time. In contrast, the environmental selection can be negative (i.e., select against a trait), in which case the trait would be eliminated over time. In either case, the more severe the selection, the more rapid the gain (or loss) of a given trait. It needs to be emphasized that polymorphisms would not be selected, for or against, if they occurred only in the elderly, or had only mild effects on the individual. This is because a disease-related polymorphism appearing in the elderly or a very mildly affecting polymorphism would not affect reproduction or child rearing and thus, would not influence overall survivability of a species. Thus, there is no selection.

As described in Chapters 4 and Appendix II, polymorphisms naturally occur in the genomes of all individuals at periodic intervals. These polymorphisms occurred while worldwide migration and geographic isolations of humans were taking place.

As select bands of humans split from one group to migrate to another geographic location, some in this migrating band developed a unique set of mutations with the associated changes in physical and metabolic/physiologic traits. They represent the founders, which are the first individuals with the new set of traits in a new colony. After the population expanded in that new location, together with positive selection, the frequency of this set of mutations (along with its traits) would expand even more rapidly. When the frequency rose to 1% in a population, the mutations would be classified as polymorphisms.

In summary, the rate of expansion of any group, whose traits give it an environmental advantage over the rest of the population, would be greater than that of other groups. Any given trait with a positive selective advantage would eventually become predominant in the population and an ethnic trait would be created. It should be mentioned that polymorphisms that cause a mild trait such as a mild disease but do not hurt reproduction or survivability of a population, would not be subjected to selection (positive or negative), since such polymorphisms would not be affected by the environmental selection process.

Skin Color

Humans tend not to see beyond skin color and appearances in general when meeting others, and it is often an issue in societies due to its high visibility. So let us discuss skin color as a positive selection advantage. Skin shades generally correlate with the latitudes where a population has resided for thousands of years. Skin shade is primarily based on the extent of the chemical compound, melanin, in the skin. As with many traits, however, many genes play a role in skin shade. A polymorphism in one of these genes, called SL C24A5, has recently been found in Europeans to be a major cause of skin lightening. Interestingly, recent analyses have also shown that there are different genes which caused skin lightening in East Asians compared to those which caused skin lightening in Europeans. Thus, Mother Nature has more than one pattern of DNA changes which result in the same trait.

As outlined in Figure 5.1, geographic locations on Earth have different environmental conditions, including sun exposure. Why does one observe that populations living closer to the equator (i.e., maximal sunlight) tend to have darker skin while the skin shade lightens in populations closer to either pole?

Figure 5.1

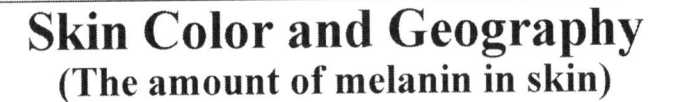

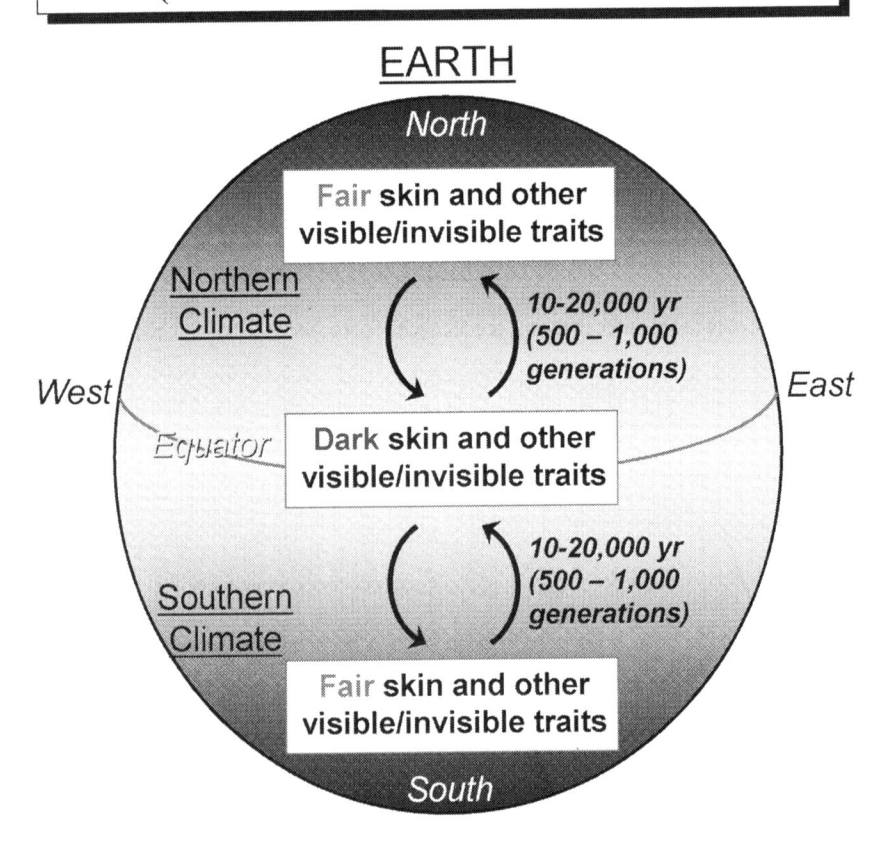

Skin Color and Geography
(The amount of melanin in skin)

EARTH

North

Fair skin and other visible/invisible traits

Northern Climate

10-20,000 yr (500 – 1,000 generations)

West

Equator

Dark skin and other visible/invisible traits

East

10-20,000 yr (500 – 1,000 generations)

Southern Climate

Fair skin and other visible/invisible traits

South

Figure 5.1 Map of the earth depicting skin color (due to melanin) by geographic region.

The cause of this environmental selection is fairly well understood. In the equatorial regions, the darker skin prevents skin damage, infections, Vitamin B destruction, cancer (e.g., melanoma), and the over-production of Vitamin D, all of which are harmful to humans. When West Africans, still residing in Africa, developed a genetic flaw in producing melanin, effectively giving them light skin, they often developed and succumbed to skin cancer at young ages. This is an example of negative environmental selection. In the far north or far south, where there is less sun and lower temperatures, those with lighter skin are favored. This is because fair skin is able to produce essential Vitamin D with less sunlight, Vitamin B destruction is not an issue, and there is no worry that the sun would damage the skin. Complete changes in skin color are speculated to require thousands of years.

Since those with lighter skin in the more Northern regions of the earth are favored for survival, their population base expands faster than others to create more fair skinned people over thousands of years. This process would reverse if fair-skinned people migrated back to the equator (Africa, India, South America, etc.) (See Figure 5.1). Some molecular anthropologists predict that it requires 250 to 1000 or so generations (e.g., 5,000-20,000 years), before environmentally favored (positive) traits would predominate in a whole population. In addition, environmentally disfavored traits would disappear. This constant genetic change and selection of the fittest encourages adaptation and thus, survival in any location.

Other Physical Features

Another visible example of positive selection is the physical features of people of Asian descent. For instance, in the Asian/Mongolian people, the features of heavy slanted eyelids are speculated to protect against the glare of the sun on snow, and their stocky physique helps protect against the cold. Anthropologists also speculate that the Asiatic/Mongolian features, such as eyelid folds, short limbs, short noses, flat faces, a low surface area to mass ratio, and large sinuses, appeared only during and after the last ice age (24,000 - 14,000 years ago) and would have helped mankind deal with the cold temperatures and snow glare in Siberia. Even seemingly minor traits such as the Mongolian/Siberian teeth, including incisors, premolars, and molars, were adapted for eating large amounts of meat and gristle. Thus, the predominance of those features occurred during the end of the last ice age (14,000 - 12,000 years ago). In the Northern regions of Asia, with its open plains, the yellowish skin (caused by excess carotene) found in many Asians arose since it allows vitamin D production with less sunlight, while protecting people in exposed plains from harmful UV light from the sun.

To summarize, when individuals move to a geographic location where a formerly favorable acquired trait is unhealthy (i.e. negative environmental selection), the individuals with that unhealthy trait would tend to be eliminated by negative environmental selection. Individuals whose polymorphisms create healthy traits which favor survival, would thrive and their numbers would expand in a population. Some polymorphic changes in the genome are simply "mild or neutral polymorphisms," i.e., they have no effect on any physical or physiologic trait and, thus, no selection by the environment. In this case, they would not be selected for or against in a population, since there is no environmental selection. These environmentally neutral polymorphisms might randomly (and more slowly) expand due to population expansion.

Examples of specific physical attributes among different ethnic populations can be found in the Olympic Records. Almost all of the top sprinting speeds are held by males and females of West Africans and of African Americans whose ancestry came from West Africa. In fact, all the finalists in the past Olympic men's 100 meter race and most of the broad jump are of West African decent. This ability is speculated to have evolved due to the need for speed in hunting animals or to escape predators by the ancestors of these athletes from West African jungles. In middle and long distance events, the men and women who descended from Kenya and Ethiopia (East Africa) are the top winners with best times. It is known that for millennia, those inhabitants walked and ran long distances for food and water in the open plains of those countries. It is interesting that recent muscle research studies have identified specific muscle structures and cell physiologies unique to the East and West Africans. The structure and function of the West African muscles are designed for strength, and the East African muscles for endurance with improved oxygen utilization.

It should be mentioned that physical appearances can be deceiving, with similarities/dissimilarities in appearance not always being accurate indicators of species similarity. Very similar looking birds on earth are often genetically different species and cannot produce fertile offspring, while humans on earth, who appear quite different, do produce fertile offspring.

The Issue of Intelligence

IQ (intelligence quotient) is another criteria often used to discriminate against and categorize ethnic groups. However, past studies in this area have now been shown to be seriously flawed, and thus, the association of ethnic groups with IQ, has not been accurately documented.

As described in his book, "Mapping Human History," Steve Olson (see references in Appendix III) describes extensive studies showing that economic status plays a major role in intelligence scores worldwide. Children and adults, regardless of ethnicity, who were well nourished, well cared for (good parenting), with good opportunities and education, overall scored better on IQ tests than even those of the same country who lived in poverty and/or without favorable advantages. The same conclusions have arisen in similar studies performed in different countries and continents. In the United States, minorities (e.g., African Americans and other groups) who are proportionately more likely to be in poverty than European Americans, usually do not score as high on intelligence tests.

Similarly, the minority Buraku youth in Japan who are discriminated against in housing, education, etc., also score less on IQ tests than the rest of the Japanese population. It is also interesting that individuals in Europe, with one African and one European parent who are not discriminated against, display IQ testing equal to those with two European parents.

In other countries, with many types of tests, people from lower economic status score lower than those in average and higher economic status, regardless of their ancestry. Peoples of non-mixed and mixed ethnic groups perform, as predicted, based on their economic status, opportunities, and their parental guidance and care, and not based on the percentage of ethnicity, nor any genetic basis. When minorities of lower economic status are given the parenting and opportunities of higher economic families, they perform as well on such tests.

In conclusion, studies on intelligence levels need to be designed to eliminate social status and economic opportunities and discrimination. Also more tests to measure mathematic versus verbal performance as well as creativity should be encouraged. Based on the extensive variability in polymorphism patterns in the genomes among individuals which was discussed earlier, the author speculates that the level of IQ as with the physical or metabolic traits, are more variable among individuals within any ethnic group/population than between ethnic groups.

Disease Susceptibility and Other Invisible Traits

In any given geographic location, other changes in traits may occur over time, some of which are invisible. Examples of such invisible traits would be physiologic or metabolic changes such as disease resistance or predisposition, muscle performance, drug metabolism, immune tolerance or responses, etc. These differences are less obvious to an observer, but have been documented by scientists, physicians, and anthropologists, and are of interest since they are involved in Individualized Medicine. These traits may be due to random side effects of the spontaneous genetic drift, or a result of differing environments in isolated populations. The latter would include different diets or exposure to different infectious pathogens and plant toxins in each ecological area. These conditions, for example, could encourage the development of different drug metabolisms in populations.

Recent interesting scientific articles (Outlined in Table 5.1 with references) describes some differences in metabolic traits, including disease predisposition, in people from different continents (Baye, et al, 2009 and others). The authors relate that over time, differences in diets, sunlight, temperature, and other physical demands would create not only visible ethnic specific traits such as skin color and musculoskeletal physique, but also invisible traits such as digestion, drug metabolism, and disease predisposition.

There are many examples of these ethnic-specific invisible traits, most notably disease predisposition. African Americans display a higher incidence of high blood pressure, asthma, and prostate cancers than non-African Americans. Hispanics and Hispanic Americans display a higher incidence of diabetes than Europeans and European-Americans. Europeans and European-Americans have a higher frequency of hemochromatosis and cystic fibrosis than the rest of the world. The Ashkenazi Jews of Eastern Europe have higher incidences of Tay Sacs and Gaucher's diseases than the rest of Europe. American Indians have a higher susceptibility to influenza, measles, and smallpox than the general American population. Japanese and

Table 5.1

Physiological Differences Among Individuals from Europe, Africa, China, and Japan

A. Continent-specific physiological / developmental functions:

    Skeletal/muscular system   Digestive system
    Connective tissue   Cardiovascular system
    Hair and skin   Drug metabolism

B. Continent-specific diseases / disorders:

    Nutrition   Cancer   Immunological
    Reproduction   Blood

However, over time, individuals within each population display up to six times greater differences among each other than those that exist between populations, due to continuing spontaneous genetic changes in each individual.

Thus, the new field of "Individualized Medicine"

Table 5.1 Physiological traits / transitions in the populations of 4 continents.
(Data taken from Baye et al 2009, Personalized Medicine, 6:623-641; Bar-bujani et al 1997, Proc Natl Acad Sci 94, 4516-4519; Olsen 2002, Mapping Human History, Houghton-Mifflen Co., New York.)

American Puma Indians have higher incidence of diabetes than others around the world.

There are many more examples of polymorphisms in ethnic-specific invisible traits. Studies described by J. K. Pritchard (see references in Appendix III) identified a gene, "LARGE," that enhances a body's ability to fight against the endemic Lassa fever virus infection. This gene has undergone recent positive natural selection in Nigeria. Polymorphisms in the gene for the lactase enzyme that digest the sugar in milk have undergone rapid expansion in Europe, Middle East, and East Africa over the past 5,000 - 10,000 years. The most rapidly recorded change in a population is a polymorphism in a gene, EPASI, which allows a more efficient utilization of oxygen at high altitudes, and which has expanded within the past 3,000 years among Chinese who migrated to Tibet. Similarly, women in high altitudes in Bolivia developed an enlarged artery (over 10,000 years ago) to help carry more oxygen to their embryos in these low oxygen environments.

In many populations in sub-Saharan Africa, a well-characterized polymorphism found in the beta globin gene of hemoglobin protects against a form of malaria. This polymorphism has become a dominant trait. When both genes have the polymorphism, it causes a deformed hemoglobin protein and deformed red blood cells; the result is the individual having sickle cell anemia, which is often fatal. In this case, the disease is a strong negative selector for continuance in a population. However, if only one of the two genes has the defect, the individual has the sickle cell trait with few symptoms such as mild anemia. They maintain a high representation in this region of Africa since the people have a selective environmental advantage, as they are resistant to malaria, which is endemic to that area and lethal to many. Thus they survive to reproduce and the sickle cell polymorphism is maintained in high frequency in Africa.

Disease resistance in certain populations is due to the exposure and selection in that population to similar diseases in the past. Due to natural selection, those with a resistance to disease survived and that resistance trait expanded in that population. Scientists, however, feel that the environment can also have immediate effects on disease susceptibility. For example, Japanese men living in Japan rarely get prostate cancer, but the incidences markedly increase when they live in the USA. Similarly, Asian women show a marked increase in breast cancer when they move to Western societies. These aspects are currently being studied, but are believed to be due to the environment, including their diet.

Individual Variations are Greater than Population Differences

As shown in Table 5.1 and indicated from the studies of Baye et al (see Appendix III), even though there are these reported differences in ethnic traits (physical and metabolic) caused by genetic (polymorphic) differences between the different continental populations (races), the overall differences are unexpectedly minor. As noted in Table 5.1, other major studies have shown that the differences among the individuals within each population are greater than those between populations [see Appendix III, Barbujani, et al, (1997) and Lewontin (1972)]. These studies have shown that, comparing the genetic variations among individuals within a population to populations from different continents/locations, much greater differences are found among individuals within a population than between one population to another. In fact, individual variations within a single population are usually 6-fold greater than those found between populations. This is due to periodic, natural, spontaneous, genetic changes causing the individual's traits to differ, over time, from other individuals within the same population. This phenomenon is the basis of a new field of medicine, Individualized Medicine, whereby we now realize that each individual in a population is somewhat unique from another, including in drug metabolism, subtypes of diseases such as cancers, susceptibility to diseases, resistance to diseases, etc. It should be mentioned that individual man-made environmental changes, such as smoking or working around toxic substances, markedly increases the rate of genomic change. As a result, an increase in disease occurrence has been found.

Conclusions

To summarize, it appears that many factors play a role in how rapidly a trait predominates in a population (see Pritchard, Appendix III). Those traits involving changes in multiple genes (polygenic) may develop more rapidly, especially in a small population. For traits that involve individual genes, the migration of people carrying that gene to different locales would have a large impact. Over extended periods of isolation of populations, differences in visible and invisible traits between individuals within each population became much greater than the trait differences between populations. Again, this phenomenon is due to natural, spontaneous genetic drift, which arises among individuals within each population. This phenomenon explains how all of our ancestors were dark skinned Africans and some ended up in Europe, Asia, and the Americas as lighter skinned inhabitants.

Chapter 6

Biology and Genetics Say We are

Only Variants of One Species

6

Biology and Genetics Say We are Only Variants of One Species

Definitions

Races: (1) A non-scientific socio-cultural term based on culture and appearance (ethnic grouping), but not on biology. An inaccurate description or explanation of human biological variation. Often used to divide people somewhat arbitrarily into ethnic groups. (2) Divisions between human populations possessing physical traits that are transmissible in offspring. (3) Communities or classes of people unified by physical or cultural traits; an interbreeding group within a species.

Racialism/Racism: Racialism is the practice of racial prejudice or discrimination. Racism is the philosophy of grouping people arbitrarily based on an individual's or society's desires to isolate one group for cultural, political, or economic reasons. It is the belief that race is the primary determinant of human traits, abilities, and capacities, and the assumption that racial differences produce an inherent superiority of one particular race over another.

Ethnicity: (1) An indigenous native population with unique or different physical, metabolic, or cultural traits; (2) Relating to populations or large groups of people classified according to common traits, language, and customs, e.g., Asian, Indian, African, etc.

Species: (1) A biological classification comprising closely related organisms or populations capable of mating and producing fertile offspring. Usually the members of this group have common attributes or physical traits and resemble each other more than individuals of other groups. (2) A group of mating individuals who do not mate with individuals of other species, but can mate among themselves and produce fertile offspring.

Variant (of a species): An individual or group of individuals within the same species, which deviates in some minor way or characteristic from others of the same species. Such differences are not due to age, sex, or social position. Variants within a species are capable of mating and producing fertile offspring.

Foundations of Racism

The term "race" is a social term used by individuals in a society to denote a variety of meanings. Some abuse this term to the extent that they dehumanize other humans, inferring that a group of others are so very different physically and/or physiologically that they are separate from one's own species and cannot assimilate into "their society."

People who support these views are "racists." The terms race, species, variants, and ethnicity are found in scientific as well as general dictionaries. However, the terms racism, racialism, and racial profiling are cultural and societal terms, are found only in general language dictionaries, and are not listed in science dictionaries (e.g., biological, medical, or genetics).

Interestingly, the definitions of race or ethnicity, taken from Webster's Dictionary, Roger's Thesaurus, and various scientific dictionaries, do not communicate any such thoughts of racism. Rather, race or ethnicity is defined as "the physical or cultural differences among the common modern man". Racialism (the practice of using racism) has been used by individuals, groups, or societies to infer that other races are inferior. In short, it is the practice of racial prejudice and discrimination.

The term "racism" is described in one dictionary as "the philosophy of categorizing people arbitrarily based on an individual's or society's desire to isolate one group for cultural, political, or financial reasons, and the belief (or rationale) that racial differences produce an inherent superiority of a particular race over another." In the past, many uninformed individuals and groups have believed that they were superior to another group based on their genetics and/or unique traits and have assumed that such minorities could never assimilate into the main society. Scientifically (biologically and genetically), they could not be more wrong.

This book has dealt with molecular and biological processes which cause human differences, as well as why and how these events occur. We have learned in the previous chapters about the human genome, the biological and genetic perspective of human origins, world migrations, and the process involved in the development of different traits, such as skin color and other physical and metabolic differences. Figure 6.1 summarizes how these traits have occurred and are still occurring. As discussed in earlier chapters, groups of humans migrated out of Africa to various geographic locations worldwide and remained

Figure 6.1

Creation of Different Traits Among Populations

Migration and Geographical Isolation

The genetic changes (initially called mutations) which spontaneously occur in individuals will expand as the population expands and become prevalent in an isolated population as polymorphisms, such as SNPs. This process creates unique ethnic traits which often differ from other distant populations.

⇩

Possible Environmental Influences / Adaptation

The expansion of these polymorphisms and resulting traits in a population are increased if the traits help individuals adapt and survive in a new environment. If the polymorphic traits hurt an individual's ability to adapt in an environment, then they are selected against and the trait often dissapears.

⇩

Isolated Population Outcome

The specific patterns of expanded genetic polymorphisms in a population cause specific physical and metabolic traits unique to that population. These include appearance, disease predispositions, disease resistance, and drug metabolism.

Figure 6.1 Chart depicting the creation of different traits among populations

geographically isolated for long periods. The process of "genetic drift," which involves the gradual appearance of naturally occurring, periodic, spontaneous genetic changes (mutations), caused changes in physical and metabolic traits in these groups. (See Appendix II) In many instances, these traits were unique to each isolated group, mostly directed by environmental selection, and ultimately created the unique physical and metabolic traits for each population. These populations were often classified as ethnic groups or races. The environment often favors one trait over another for survival, a process called "adaptation," resulting in a more rapid and greater increase in the changes within the populations. Combining these processes with cultural differences (of language, customs, etc.), one can speculate how certain people develop a strong opinion that humans who differ in physical appearance might also have major biological and genetic differences.

Humans Belong to a Single Species

The biological and genetic evidence of the common relationships and ancestry that all humans share, combined with the fact that all humans on earth can and have co-mingled (mated) and reproduced viable offspring, no matter what the ethnic group, proves, by definition of species, that all humans on the earth are of the same species. The differences that occur among human populations are minor physical or metabolic traits when comparing humans to other animal species, including monkeys. The scientific conclusion is that different ethnic groups (races) are only variants of the same species. The physical differences simply generated by natural, spontaneous genetic changes established by "Mother Nature," allow humans to adapt to environmental changes, including both naturally occurring and those which appear when populations migrate to different geographic locations. The cultural differences are simply social habits which are generated in each isolated population.

Scientists predict that environmental selection could, over time, even reverse many of the "adaptive traits" incurred previously by humans. In short, over time, humans can "re-adapt" or even reverse back to previous traits. As discussed in the previous chapter, and as depicted in Figure 5.1, for the sake of survival, natural, environmentally selected changes would reverse the skin color as well as other physical and metabolic traits if a population moved to a different location which favored that change.

Due to spontaneous genetic drift, racial features (both external and internal), are not "permanent" in a species, but can change (and are changing) in one direction or another. The mingling (mating) of different ethnic groups can and does rapidly alter any trait. As stated in Chapter 5, a trait can be positively or negatively selected. It could also not be selected at all, if the traits caused by the polymorphisms are not affected by the environment. In this case, the trait would only expand as the population expands, at the same steady level in the population.

Humans are All Related

It is important to remind ourselves that all humans originated from Africa (i.e., are African) and all are related, so every person you know or meet is a distant cousin, at one level or another. Table 6.1 summarizes some of the interesting facts on physical and metabolic traits that occur within a population due to genetic drift and environmental selection. Figure 6.2 shows that in the past 200 years (or 10 generations ago), each person has a thousand direct ancestors. Going back 20-25 generations, each

Table 6.1

Human Races as per Molecular Anthropology

1. All humans on earth do not belong to different species, as all humans can reproduce. Humans are variants of the same species. Humans only have mild genomic differences which are often environmentally determined.
2. All humans on earth are all or part African and are related.
3. Purity of race does not exist. All populations mixed with others wherever they coexisted.
4. All populations have some genetic weaknesses and strengths.
5. Ethnicity may be a better term than race since the latter has been so abused by societies.
6. It takes 10,000 to 20,000 years (500-1,000 generations) for any given environmentally selected ethnic trait, such as skin color, to develop or to be reversed under changing conditions.
7. Recent genomic analyses of 4 ethnic groups (European, African, Chinese, Japanese) support other medical studies that some functional continental (population specific) differences exist.
8. However, individuals within a population display up to six fold greater variation than between populations.
9. This individual variation within a population includes physical appearances and metabolic and physiologic processes, which has created the need for "Individualized Medicine".

Table 6.1 A molecular anthropologist's view of the human race.

Figure 6.2

Theoretical Calculations of Human Generations (20 years / generation) and our Ancestry

Generations	Years ago (from 2010)	Number of ancestors
3	60 (1950 AD)	8
5	100 (1910 AD)	32
8	160 (1850 AD)	256
*10	200 (1810 AD)	10^3 (thousand)
*15	300 (1710 AD)	3×10^4 (30 thousand)
20	400 (1610 AD)	10^6 (1 million)
**25	500 (1510 AD)	30×10^6 (30 million)
30	600 (1410 AD)	10^9 (1 billion)
40	800 (1210 AD)	10^{12} (1 trillion)

*People with geographic or religious barriers for mating (marriages) are likely to have common ancestors 200-300 years ago (10-15 generations; theoretically 30,000 ancestors).

**Everyone now is related to everyone else within a reasonable geographic area. Even immigrant people of common origin (Europe, Asia, etc.) are likely to have common ancestors 500 years ago (25 generations; theoretically 30 million [30×10^6] ancestors).

Figure 6.2 Theoretical calculations depicting the number of ancestors at various past generations.

of us has approximately a million ancestors and over the past 30-40 generations, each of us has billions of ancestors. These numbers do not even include the fact that people live beyond 20 years (child bearing age) and have multiple children. From these calculations, it is evident that all humans are cousins at some level. In isolated communities of only a few thousand inhabitants, all would be directly related within 10-15 generations (approximately 200 to 300 years). In summary, humans around the world are all genetic variants of the same species. We are all African, all related, and like many of our pet dogs, all energetic mongrels.

Foundations of Individualized Medicine

Recent genetic analyses have revealed that spontaneous genetic drift creates much greater differences among individuals within the same population than differences between populations (discussed in Chapter 5). As stated earlier, this process is the foundation of the new Personalized/Individualized Medicine which has been recently recognized by the medical field. Individualized medicine is founded on the knowledge that each person, in addition to their unique physical appearance, has a unique physiology and metabolism, including unique drug metabolism, disease resistance, and disease susceptibility.

Chapter 7

The Myth of Race

7

The Myth of Race

The new fields of Medical Genomics and Molecular Anthropology have revealed, even more strongly, that all humans on earth are of the same species with minor differences (ethnic variants). They have revealed how humans became variants of one species, as outlined in this book. Lastly, the genomics field has shown that we are all African, all related, all mongrels, and one could say, have all originated from the same human population in Africa.

How racism arose in human history is described in the first chapter. Its very basis and survival in the face of the new science of Molecular Genetics and Anthropology can now be challenged on a scientific basis. Genomic analyses have shown that there is no "pure" human or race, no standard bearer, and no "best" human individual, population, or race on the earth.

Those of us living today have changed from our ancient ancestors. We are continually changing and adapting. Siblings from the same parents have been shown to differ from each other by 100 genetic markers (polymorphisms) when born. Even identical twins have been shown to differ from each other by a few genetic markers when born. This process is due to genetic drift in each person's genome over time.

We have to acknowledge that there are a variety of issues regarding racial prejudices. Among many individuals, there may be, in part, a fundamental need to believe they are superior to others who are different from themselves. Many, if not all, of these racial philosophies are learned behaviors/opinions, usually knowingly or unknowingly taught by parents and society to the young. The practice of racism by individuals, and sometimes by a whole society, is often based on the desire for some form of personal benefit. Historically, racism has been used not only to promote feelings of superiority, but also to blame others for bad economic or social situations, or as an excuse to take advantage of another group. In short, a racist's view that some human ethnic groups are subhuman (less than human), is due to a lack of knowledge of the biologic and genetic facts.

One might argue the possibility that there is some lingering ancestral urge in humans to distrust those different from ourselves. This ancient ancestral instinct to fear "foreigners" (different humans) could be due to the fact that, in the ancient and not too ancient past, the arrival of uninvited, different appearing or different speaking peoples often meant danger of "attack." These "immigrants" could have attacked for food, possessions, mates, or to enslave the native people. The alarms arising from any such incursions of different peoples were often justified for survival.

Possibly, we humans today have maintained some of these deep ancestral fears and feelings of distrust of "foreigners." Thus, such fears of "different looking people" may be instinctive. Evidence has substantiated that such fears and prejudices leading to racism are also learned behaviors. With our current knowledge about the biology and genetics of our ancestry, humans today should be able to logically assess and negate such fears. Education, knowledge, and awareness are the best means by which to eliminate racial prejudices.

Regarding populations as a whole, the physiologic/metabolic variations between different ethnic groups, based on inherited polymorphisms, have been shown to have some specific geographical distribution around the world. Many metabolic patterns and disease predispositions are different from population to population. However, as described in the previous chapter, Geneticists and Anthropologists are also learning that individuals within a population are even more diverse from each other than are individuals between populations. Thus, the field of Personalized (Individualized) Medicine has been created to deal with individual differences in medical related disposition and therapies. We now understand how and why these differences have occurred.

No individual on this earth is without genetic mutations or weaknesses in physiology, which are often the basis of organ dysfunction. So - who on this earth is better than anyone else? Humans tend not to look beyond surface features, but such criteria are misleading. All humans worldwide, who look quite different, belong to the same species and differ from each other only by less than 0.1% at the genetic level, and can produce fertile offspring.

Similarly, all of the markedly different breeds of dogs around the world belong to the same species and can produce viable offspring. In contrast, very similar looking birds are often of different species and cannot reproduce.

The genetically closest living creature to humans, the primates, contain 20 to 50 times (depending on the primate) greater genetic differences from humans than found among all humans on the earth. Other mammals have hundreds of fold greater genetic differences from humans than found among all humans around the world. With the current knowledge of biology and genomics, humans today have little excuse for practicing racism. Thus, the Myth of Race (as we have come to know it). We humans all belong to the same species, we are variants of the one species, all related, all African, and all mongrels. Our DNA defines who we really are and where we all came from.

Glossary

Archeology: Study of life and culture of the past, ancient peoples, relics, tools, architecture.

Bases and base pairs: Bases are the four chemical compounds abbreviated (A, T, G, and C) which, in a series, carry the genetic information which determines human physical appearance and metabolism. These are the letters in the language of life. These bases, in a long series, contain the genetic information that the cell uses, in groups called "genes." The cell uses this genetic information to assemble proteins to create and maintain each human body. Bases are bound as pairs (G-C and A-T) in the double-stranded DNA molecule and serve as genetic markers in genetics.

Chromosome: A thread-like structure found in the nuclei of most living cells consisting of multi-folded/compacted DNA strands carrying the genetic information as DNA (genes).

DNA (Deoxyribonucleic Acid): The genetic material found in the cell nucleus carries the genetic information as "genes." It consists of two thin threads of sugars (polysaccharides) bound to each other side by side via pairing of bases (base pairs) which are bound to the sugars.

DNA sequencing: A laboratory technique for determining the exact sequence, i.e., order of occurrence, of the 4 known bases that are abbreviated by the letters G, C, A, and T.

Ethnicity: (1) An indigenous native population with unique or different physical, metabolic, or cultural traits; (2) Relating to populations or large groups of people classified according to common traits, language, and customs, e.g., Asian, Indian, African, etc.

Gene: A distinct sequence (region) of DNA found in chromosomes, whose base sequence codes for proteins which, in turn, determines the traits/properties of a human being and is inherited. Humans have a total of 20,000 to 25,000 genes, which are inherited, i.e., are passed on to subsequent generations.

Generation: The time required for a newborn baby to mature to generate another baby. In this book a generation is assumed to be 20 years.

Genetic Drift: The periodic, spontaneous changes over time in our DNA, some of which ultimately can cause changes in appearances/physiology in isolated populations which ultimately creates differences between populations (ethnic groups).

Haplogroups: A large group of people who share the same vast, but unique, polymorphism patterns. Each group contains several to many related haplotypes and are used to define branches of the tree depicting early human origins and ancestry.

Haplotype: The individual pattern of genetic markers (polymorphisms) found in the DNA of individual humans which categorizes them with other related family members. Some represent more recently created markers used to identify recent relatives. Thus, individuals with the same haplotype are closely related and the more different the haplotype, the more distantly they are related. These haplotype patterns have been studied on either the male Y chromosomal DNA, or the female mitochondrial DNA.

Human Genome Project: The complete analysis of human DNA (genetic information) that required 10 years and 3 billion dollars to complete. The project involved the sequencing (determining the order) of 3 billion bits of information along the DNA. These bits of information are called base pairs.

Human Genome: Taken from the Greek language, refers to all DNA (genes) in all the chromosomes of an organism. In humans, this consists of the DNA in all 23 pairs of chromosomes in the cell nucleus, as well as DNA in a cell organelle called the mitochondria (see definition below).

Mitochondria: Energy producing bodies in all human cells which contain their own DNA packaged as a small chromosome. All mitochondria and their DNA are inherited only from the mother (female inheritance), so both the boys and girls inherit the mother's mitochondrial DNA. However, only the girls pass on their particular mitochondrial DNA to subsequent generations. Thus, this mitochondrial DNA and its polymorphisms are used to trace female lineages (see Figure 4.1) (see Note 7, Appendix I. for added information).

Molecular Anthropology: The study of mankind, comparing their physical characteristics (from physical anthropology) and habitats with differences in their DNA (genome).

Mutation: A rare, spontaneous change in the genetic markers (i.e., change in the sequence of bases), which is passed on to subsequent generations. This usually occurs in <.001% of the population. During cell replication, the DNA is replicated and passed on to the daughter cell. Mutations are errors created in the DNA during DNA replication, called "mutations," which are also passed on with the rest of the DNA to future generations. The process occurs spontaneously, and ultimately causes "Genetic Drift" in populations. The process occurs in one or a few individuals and can expand in frequency in a population to become a polymorphism.

<u>Physical Anthropology</u>: Study of mankind through their physical and cultural characteristics, their customs and social relationships, etc.

<u>Physical traits</u>: Visible features like eye color, hair structure, nose shape, and other features which are determined by inherited genes from our parents.

<u>Physiological/metabolic traits</u>: Invisible features relating to the physiology and metabolism/chemistry of an individual, including disease predisposition, which are also determined by inherited genes from our parents.

<u>Polymorphism</u>: A term used when mutations increase in numbers to approximately 1% or more of the population. As the population expands, changes in polymorphisms (base sequence changes) often create changes in human traits. These changes occur

spontaneously and periodically and their appearance can be roughly dated and represent the foundations of "Genetic Drift" in populations.

(see Appendix I, Notes 1 and 2, for additional details.)

Races: (1) A non-scientific socio-cultural term based on culture and appearance (ethnic grouping), but not on biology. An inaccurate description or explanation of human biological variation. Often used to divide people somewhat arbitrarily into ethnic groups. (2) Divisions between human populations possessing physical traits that are transmissible in offspring. (3) Communities or classes of people unified by physical or cultural traits; an interbreeding group within a species.

Racialism/Racism: Racialism is the practice of racial prejudice or discrimination. Racism is the philosophy of grouping people arbitrarily based on an individual's or society's desires to isolate one group for cultural, political, or economic reasons. It is the belief that race is the primary determinant of human traits, abilities, and capacities, and the assumption that racial differences produce an inherent superiority of one particular race over another.

Species: (1) A biological classification comprising closely related organisms or populations capable of mating and producing fertile offspring. Usually the members of this group have common attributes or physical traits and resemble each other more than individuals of other groups. (2) A group of mating individuals who do not mate with individuals of other species, but can mate among themselves and produce fertile offspring.

Variant (of a species): An individual or group of individuals within the same species, which deviates in some minor way or characteristic from others of the same species. Such differences are not due to age, sex, or social position. Variants within a species are capable of mating and producing fertile offspring.

X chromosome: One of two sex chromosomes containing genes which determine the gender of an individual. Two X chromosomes, each donated from the father and mother, create a female. One X chromosome from the mother and one Y chromosome from the father create a male.

Y chromosome: One of the two sex chromosomes containing genes which determine the gender of an individual. Inherited only from the father (male inheritance). Used to trace male (father) lineages. The male (carrying an X and a Y) thus determines the sex of any offspring by donating either an X or a Y to the mother's X chromosome for the child (see Figure 4.1).

Note: See Appendix I, Notes 1 and 2, for more detailed description/definitions of important genetic terminology.

Appendix I

Notes for Further Reading

The following represents notes and figures removed from earlier versions of the text which may be of interest to certain readers.

NOTE 1: Expanded Definitions

DNA (DEOXYRIBONUCLEIC ACID): The chemical name of the molecule, a nucleic acid, that contains the genes packaged in the cell nucleus as one long double strand of connecting sugars (polysaccharides), and highly folded into chromosomes. The DNA molecule consists of two long strands of connecting sugars with structures, called bases, protruding from each sugar in the polysaccharide strand. The bases on one strand pair with the bases on the other strand so the two strands line up along side each other connected by these bases. The sequence of these bases in certain areas of each strand carries the genetic information. (See Figure 4.1 in Chapter 4 for a model depicting the cell, chromosomes, and DNA).

GENE: The basic physical unit of inheritance, coding for proteins and RNA needed for life. Genes are passed from parents to offspring. Genes are located along the strands of the DNA in the chromosomes as a sequence of bases (genetic code). Genes contain the genetic information to specify protein structures whose functions ultimately determine various human "traits." As there are two matching chromosomes, so there are two matching genes for each trait. Hundreds to thousands of genes are found in each of the chromosomes.

RNA (RIBONUCLEIC ACID): The chemical name for another type of nucleic acid, which is different from DNA in sugar composition. This molecule serves in cell structure, as a regulator of gene activity, and as a mediator in the transfer of genetic information from the DNA to protein. RNA is a single-stranded nucleic acid with a similar structure to a single DNA strand and is synthesized using the DNA as a template. Most RNA species serve to transfer the genetic information from DNA to proteins.

GENE EXPRESSION/ACTIVITY: Gene expression is the process of the transfer of genetic information from DNA to RNA (called transcription or RNA synthesis) and from RNA to proteins (called translation or protein synthesis). Gene activity refers to the rate of this exchange, or in essence, the rate of synthesis of RNA or protein.

NON-CODING DNA: DNA regions (sequences of bases) that do not code for proteins or RNA, and are often between genes.

PROTEIN: A major class of molecules whose structure and function are determined by the genes, and are essential for life in all living organisms. Each protein represents a long chain of amino acids whose series order (sequence) is determined by the base sequence in the DNA genes. This genetic information is transcribed from DNA to RNA and "translated" from RNA into the protein.

NOTE 2: Structure of the Human Genome

Genes are those domains that code for proteins (see Figure 1 - Appendix I) such as skin proteins, muscle proteins, connective tissue proteins, and enzymes (functional active proteins). Approximately 20,000 to 25,000 genes, representing 2% of the total DNA (genome), code for structures that create the complex human body. Another 8% of the genome codes for structural RNAs involved in protein synthesis, while the rest of the genome (90%) was originally termed "junk" DNA. The bulk of this DNA is now known to harbor heretofore, unrecognized "active" genes coding for small RNA molecules or for small peptides which regulate gene expression, and protein production and processing. Some of these have now even been found to play important roles in human diseases. The remaining junk DNA has been found to contain: 1) ancient, now unused, genes (pseudogenes); 2) ancient viral sequences, such as transposons, that infected humans many thousands of years ago; and 3) repeat sequences often inserted into the DNA.

Figure 1- Appendix I

Composition of the Human Genome
(From the Human Genome Project)

100% of Genome = ~ 20,000 to 30,000 active genes

⇩

<u>% of the Genome (DNA)</u>:
~2% = Code for Proteins (~100,000 different types)
   (~ Half are of unknown specific function)
~8% = Code for Structural RNAs
~90% = Unknown (Junk DNA?)
- Introns (within genes)
- Intergenic regions (between genes)
- Ancient Transposable/Viral genes
- Ancient/Discarded Genes (Pseudogenes)
- Junk DNA contains transcribable units
  In a new breakthrough, it appears that ~50% of junk DNA is transcribed (active); The generated "<u>Small-RNAs</u>" regulate approximately half of the protein coding genes via several mechanisms.

<u>Figure 1 (Appendix I)</u> Composition of the human genome.

NOTE 3

Table I (Appendix I) lists a few examples of the dozen or so estimated human species (hominids) that have been described by Physical Anthropologists. It is estimated that about one million years ago, after spending approximately 700,000 years migrating around Africa, Homo erectus migrated out of Africa to the Middle East and Asia. Neanderthals, appearing in Africa approximately 600,000 years ago, migrated out of Africa approximately 400,000 years ago to populate the Middle East, Europe, and Western Asia. They became extinct approximately 30,000 years ago, overlapping modern humans (Homo sapiens) in Europe for 10,000 years and in other regions overlapping for up to 30,000 years. Figure 2 (Appendix I) shows a world map of the suspected migrations and habitats of the two predominant hominids that preceded modern humans, Homo erectus and Neanderthals. These two are believed to have overlapped each other as well. The extent to which Homo erectus, Neanderthal, and Homo sapiens, communicated, ignored each other, or made war, is unknown. However, recent genomic analyses of Neanderthal DNA from ancient bones strongly supports that approximately 70,000 - 80,000 years ago in the Middle East, very early modern

Table 1 - Appendix I

History of Humans via Anthropology (Skeletal Remains)

- 8.0 MYA – Ramapithecus (Hominids and apes separate)
- 4.4 MYA – Ardipithecus ramadus (First documented Hominid species)
- 3.7 MYA – Australopethecus afarensis
- 2.5 MYA – Homo habilis (First stone tools)
- 1.7 MYA – 200,000 YA – Homo erectus
- 1.0 MYA – Homo erectus migrates out of Africa
- 500,000 YA – Neanderthal
- 350,000 YA – Neanderthal migrates out of Africa
- 200,000 YA – Homo sapiens (Modern Human)
- 50,000 YA – Homo sapiens migrates out of Africa
- 30,000 YA – Neanderthal disappears

(MYA = Million [10^6] Years Ago)

Table 1 (Appendix I) List of examples of pre-human species and dates of earliest existence.

Figure 2 - Appendix I

Migrations of Archaic Humans Out of Africa via Anthropology
(1.8 Million to 30,000 YA)

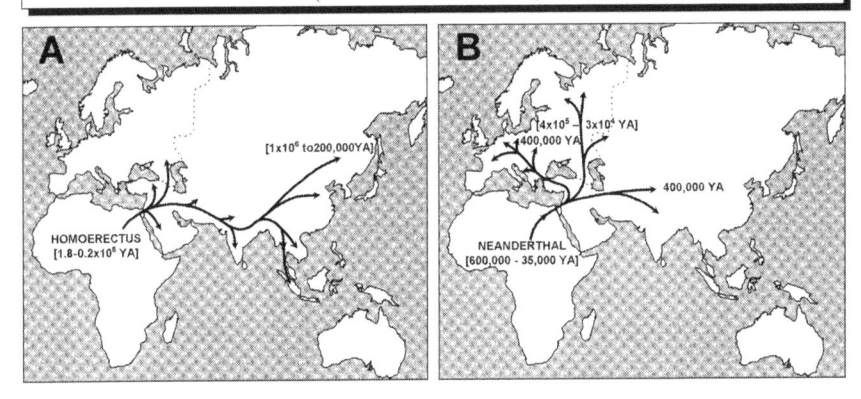

A — HOMOERECTUS [1.8-0.2x10^6 YA]; [1x10^6 to 200,000 YA]

B — NEANDERTHAL [600,000 - 35,000 YA]; [4x10^5 – 3x10^4 YA] 400,000 YA; 400,000 YA

Figure 2 (Appendix I) World map depicting the periods and directions of archaic humans out of Africa. (YA = Years Ago); (Data taken from Wells, 2006, Deep Ancestry, Inside the Genographic Project, Natl Geo., Washington, DC).

humans (Homo sapiens) migrating out of Africa did mate and produce fertile offspring with Neanderthals. Recent evidence of their DNA signature is still found in the Y chromosome of non-African human males around the world. About this same time, another archaic human species, the "Denisovans," in Siberia, also bred with modern human migrants. Recent studies in 2010 have found that 4-6% of the DNA of people in New Guinea contains this archaic human DNA.

NOTE 4: Structure of the DNA

Regarding the molecular structure of DNA, the untwisting of the DNA thread displays two strands of sugar backbone bound together by compounds called nucleotide bases, with an A (adenine) bound to a T (thymidine) and a G (guanidine) bound to a C (cytidine). Our genes represent domains coding for RNA and proteins and are located at specific sites along each DNA strand.

NOTE 5: Creation of Mutations

Mutations are rare, occurring in approximately 0.001% to 0.1% of a population. DNA polymorphisms, in contrast, begin as mutations but are reclassified when the base sequence changes occur in much higher frequency, in approximately 1% or more of the population. Mutations represent the foundation of genetic drift.

How do mutations occur? Mutations first occur as spontaneous rare changes in the DNA base pairs (less than one in one thousand or less), at roughly equivalent periodic intervals throughout the genome. Mutations usually occur when the DNA is replicating during cell proliferation. The DNA replication is highly accurate, but at consistent intervals, errors (mutations) occur.

NOTE 6: Variable Mutation Rates at Different Locations along the DNA

As demonstrated in Figure 3 (Appendix I), it should be mentioned that some regions of the genome end up having a more rapid mutation rate (higher rates of change) than other regions. Thus, some domains of our DNA, with a slow rate of polymorphic change, are used to track ancient ancestry, while the DNA with more rapid rates of change are used to track recent ancestry.

Figure 3 - Appendix I

Using Polymorphisms (SNPs) from Different Genomic Sites to Track Origins and Ancestry

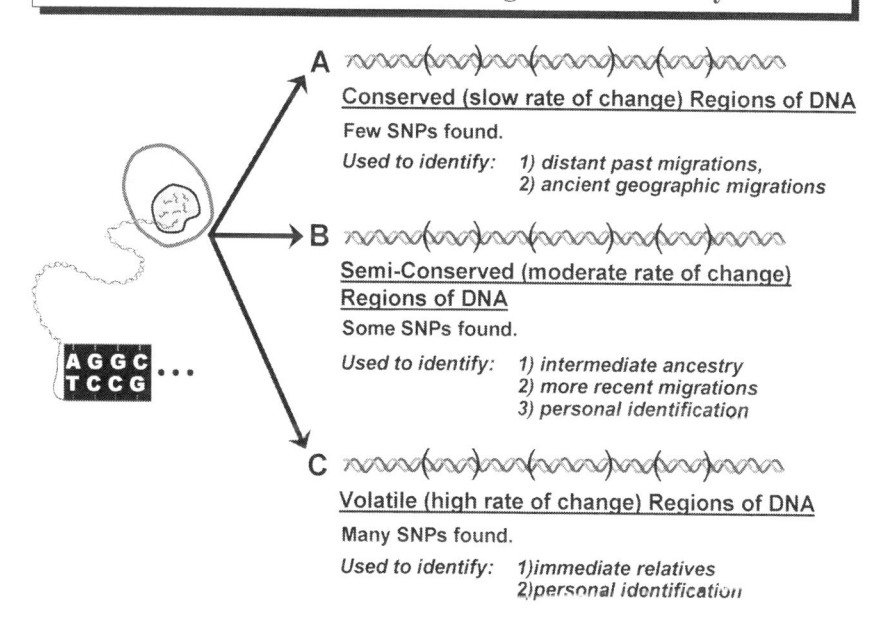

A
Conserved (slow rate of change) Regions of DNA
Few SNPs found.
Used to identify: 1) distant past migrations,
2) ancient geographic migrations

B
Semi-Conserved (moderate rate of change) Regions of DNA
Some SNPs found.
Used to identify: 1) intermediate ancestry
2) more recent migrations
3) personal identification

C
Volatile (high rate of change) Regions of DNA
Many SNPs found.
Used to identify: 1) immediate relatives
2) personal identification

Figure 3 (Appendix I) Differential rates of polymorphism (SNP) formation at different regions of the chromosome.

NOTE 7: Mitochondria

Mitochondria are hundreds of spherical organelles in each of our cells, outside the cell nucleus. These organelles are believed to have originated as bacteria that entered our cells in a symbiotic relationship approximately 2.5 billion years ago. They function to produce chemical energy for the cell. Each mitochondria contains a small circular chromosome containing only 37 or so genes. These are inherited only from the mother (female inheritance), because the male sperm mitochondria do not enter the egg during fertilization.

Appendix II

Expanded Discussions on Mutations, Polymorphisms, Adaptations, and Genetic Drift

Definitions

Mutations: Rare changes in the genetic information. A change in genetic composition (structure) which is often passed on to subsequent generations. A sudden, random change in the genetic material of a cell that, compared to non-mutated cells, potentially can cause this cell, and all cells derived from it, to differ in appearance or function. These occur at a constant low frequency during DNA replication. The most frequently occurring mutations are the single base changes (single nucleotides) called SNPs ("SNIPS") with the remaining being insertions and deletions (collectively called indels) or copy number repeats/variants (CNV) (see Figures 3.2 and 4.2 for examples).

DNA Polymorphisms (PM): Mutations that occur in over 1% of the population because of population expansion.

Genetic Drift: The periodic, spontaneous changes over time in our DNA, some of which ultimately can cause changes in appearances and physiology in isolated populations, and ultimately create differences between populations (ethnic groups).

As stated earlier, spontaneous, ever increasing, changes in our genes caused by DNA mutations and eventually polymorphisms, create gradually increasing differences in individuals' genetic markers over time (genetic drift). As depicted in Figure 1 (Appendix II), the genes in all humans on Earth are 99.9% similar to each other. The differences among humans are due to differences in the base sequences which originally occur as rare mutations, but which are reclassified as polymorphisms when their frequency expands in a population (see Appendix I, Notes 5 and 6, for further details). Figure 2 (Appendix II) shows examples of mutations/polymorphisms. As depicted in Figure 2, the major portion (~95%) of these polymorphisms are single base changes called single nucleotide polymorphisms or SNPs (pronounced "SNIPS").

Figure 1 - Appendix II

What Makes Us Humans Different

"There is 99.9 % homology among all humans on Earth."
"Only 0.1 % of the DNA bases are different."
"0.003 % actually involved in the differences in human individuality"

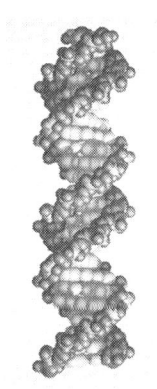

Figure 1 (Appendix II) Comparative genomics of four individual humans.

Figure 2 - Appendix II

Types of Polymorphisms (PMs)

I. <u>Single Nucleotide Polymorphism (SNP)</u>

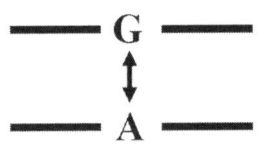

— G —
↕
— A —

95% of total PMs; ave = 1 SNP/100 bp

3% of these SNPs are functional, or cause a difference.

II. <u>Insertion / Deletions (indels)</u>

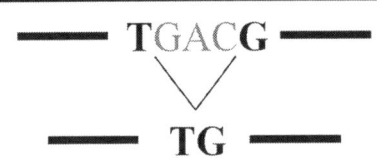

— TGACG —
∨
— TG —

Can involve thousands of bp / chromosome segment

III. <u>Copy Number Variants (CNVs)</u>

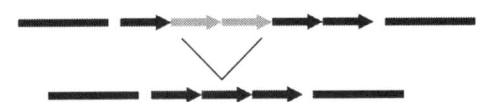

Gain or loss of >500 bp segments alters:
1) <u>Physical traits</u>, e.g., eye, hair, skin color
2) <u>Disease susceptibility</u>, e.g., autism, AIDS, Alzheimers, Parkinsons, deformities
3) <u>Drug responses</u>

<u>Figure 2 (Appendix II)</u> Types of Polymorphisms (bp = base pairs).

These are sometimes referred to as "genetic markers." The remaining 5% are represented by changes in larger DNA fragments involving many bases, which involve deletions or insertions (indels) of pieces of DNA as well as segments repeated multiple times [Copy Number Variants (CNV)].

Within an individual's genome, mutations occur naturally and spontaneously at specific intervals over time through a process called "genetic drift." This phenomenon begins even before birth. Thus, even the genomes of identical twins (from one egg) can have different genetic markers (sequences) as adults. The occurrence of mutations, which can be either good or bad for the individual, can be further increased or decreased, respectively, in a population by environmental selection. Mutations can occur at an enhanced rate because of factors in the environment, including sunlight, temperature, chemical exposure (oxidants and toxins), infectious agents, radiation, and toxic dietary foods, etc. Figure 3 (Appendix II) shows a representation of how one set of mutations would expand in an uninterrupted population to become a polymorphism. This reclassification of a mutation to a polymorphism occurs when approximately 1% or more of a population has this mutation. Considering 20 year generation

Figure 3 - Appendix II

Rapid Expansion of a Mutation to a Polymorphism in a Population
(Assuming 4 Surviving Children per Family)

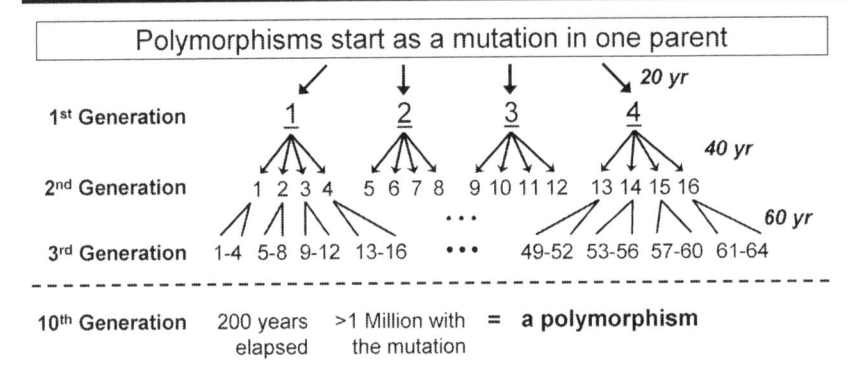

Polymorphisms start as a mutation in one parent

				20 yr
1st Generation	1	2	3	4
				40 yr
2nd Generation	1 2 3 4	5 6 7 8	9 10 11 12	13 14 15 16
		...		60 yr
3rd Generation	1-4 5-8 9-12 13-16	...	49-52 53-56	57-60 61-64

10th Generation   200 years elapsed   >1 Million with the mutation   =   **a polymorphism**

Figure 3 (Appendix II)   Rapid expansion of a mutation to a polymorphism during expansions of population.

periods with four surviving children per generation (Figure 3), any given set of mutations in the original parents would significantly expand in that population. Such a population would theoretically expand to over a million offspring with those mutations by the 10th generation. At some generation number, this increase in the frequency of a mutation in a population would reach 1% of the population and would then be classified as a polymorphism.

The constant appearance of polymorphisms, due to genetic drift, occurs in all living organisms. The rate of such changes in polymorphisms depends on three types of selection: 1) biological, reproductive, or environmental, 2) the species of animal, and 3) the size of the population. Environmental selection results in positive selection if the change is beneficial to an organism. The frequency of that polymorphism will then increase in that population. The opposite would occur if the change is deleterious to an organism.

Secondly, the rate of change of polymorphisms also depends on the species of the animal, since different animal species have different rates/frequencies of occurrences, as well as frequency and numbers of offspring. The rate of change in the DNA also differs at different locales within our genome in each animal species, including humans (see Appendix I, Note 7, for further details). Finally, using simple math, a mutation or polymorphism will increase and become dominant more rapidly in a small population than a large one.

Appendix III

References, Resources, and Further Readings

Akazawa, T. and Sathmary, E.J.E., 1996, Prehistoric Mongoloid Dispersals. Oxford University Press, New York

Alberts, Bruce, et al, 1997, Essential Cell Biology. Garland Press, New York

Avise, John C., 2010, Inside the Human Genome, Oxford University Press, New York

Barbujani, et al, 1997, An Appointment of Human DNA Diversity. Proc. Natl. Acad. Sci. 94:4516-4519

Baye, T.M., Wilke, R.A., Olivier, M. Genomic and Geographic Distribution of Private SNPs and Pathways in Human Populations. Personalized Medicine 6(6):623-641, 2009.

Burdon, R.H., 1999, Genes and the Environment, USA Taylor and Francis, Inc., Philadelphia, PA

Cameron, David W. and and Groves, Colin P., 2004, Bones, Stones and Molecules, Elsevier Academic Press, New York

Cavalli-Sforza, Luigi Luca and Cavalli-Sforza, Francesco, 1995, Great Human Diasporas, Perseus Books, New York

Cavalli-Sforza, Luigi Luca, 2000, Genes, Peoples and Languages, University of California Press, Los Angeles, CA

DeSalle, Rob and Tattersall, Ian, 2008, Human Origins, Texas A&M University Press, College Station

Fagan, Brian, 2010, Cro-Magnon: How the Ice Age gave Birth to the First Modern Humans, Bloomsbury Publishing, PLC, New York

Fredrickson, G.M., 2002, Racism: A Short History. Princeton University Press, Princeton, NJ

Jones, S., Martin, R. Pilbeam, D., and Bunney S., 1992, Cambridge Encyclopedia of Human Evolution. Cambridge University Press, New York

Koenig, Barbara, Soo-Jin Lee, Sandra, and Richardson, Sarah S, 2008, Revisiting Race in a Genomic Age. Rutgers University Press, New Brunswick, NJ.

Lewin, Roger, 1998, The Origin of Modern Humans, Scientific American Library, New York

Lewontin, R.C. 1972, The Apportionment of Human Diversity. Evol. Biol. 6:381-398

Marks, Jonathan, 2002, What it Means to be 98% Chimpanzee, University of California Press, Los Angeles, CA

Olson, Steve, 2002, Mapping Human History, Houghton Mifflin Co., New York

Palmer, Douglas, 2006, Seven Million Years, Orion Publishing Group, London

Pritchard, J.K. 2010, How We are Evolving. Sci. American, October, pp. 41-47.

Shubin, Neil, 2008, Your Inner Fish, Pantheon Books, New York

Smith, C. and Davies, E.T., 2008, Anthropology for Dummies, Wiley Publishing co., Hoboken, NJ

Smolenyak, Megan & Turner, Ann, 2004, Trace Your Roots with DNA, Rodale, Inc., New York

Sykes, Bryan (Ed), 1999, The Human Inheritance, Oxford University Press, Oxford, UK

Sykes, Bryan, 2001, Seven Daughters of Eve, W. W. Norton Co., New York

Sykes, Bryan, 2006, Saxons, Vikings and Celts, W. W. Norton Co., New York

Wade, Nicholas, 2006, Before the Dawn, Penguin Books, New York

Wells, Spencer, 2002, A genetic Odyssey, Princeton University Press, Princeton, NJ

Wells, Spencer, 2003, The Journey of Man, Random House, New York

Wells, Spencer, 2006, Deep Ancestry, Inside the Genographic Project, National Geographic Society, Washington, DC

Appendix IV

Some Interesting Facts about Human History

- About 81 billion humans have ever lived or are alive
- For every person alive today, only 12 have died.
- Modern humans have existed for 10,000 generations (200,000 years). Only 3-4,000 generations have passed since our ancestors migrated out of Africa.
- Within 10,000 or so years after modern humans encountered pre-modern humans, e.g., homo erectus in Asia, and Neanderthal in Asia/Europe, pre-modern humans disappeared.
- Recent genomic analyses have determined that Neanderthals and modern humans did interbreed approximately 70,000 - 80,000 years ago, in the Middle East, shortly after the latter left Africa.
- Due to interbreeding and religious conversions, there are no genetic markers that can assign any individual to any particular religion.

Appendix V

Getting Your Genes Analyzed

National Geographic Mag: $100 – will analyze your ancestors out of Africa to "Europe?" up to approximately 10,000 years ago
WWW3.nationalgeographic.com/genographic/participate.html

23 and Me: For genealogy and inherited susceptibility
WWW.23andme.com

Navigenics: Matches your gene sequences with current medical research and genetic risk
WWW.navigenics.com

The DNA Ancestry Project: For ethnic and geographic origins
WWW.DNAAncestryProject.com

Discover Your Ancestry: For ethnic and geographic origins
WWW.AncestrybyDNA.com

Genetrack DNA Testing: For ethnic and geographic origins
WWW.genetrackus.com

Trace Genetics: For ethnic and geographic origins
WWW.tracegenetics.com

DNA Geneology Test: For ethnic and geographic origins
WWW.dnaancestry.com

Made in the USA
Lexington, KY
19 March 2011